Bloody Amazing

123 taboo smashing poems

…It's About Bleeding Time

Kate Noakes

Bloody Amazing...

... collecting these poems has been. It all began when one of us wrote a great lament about the menopause on FaceBook, and the other said, you know what, this is the start of an anthology, only let's include premenopausal joys too.

Because we knew that loads of us women have back ache, front ache, headache, but weary and teary as hell though we are, still we go on. Pass exams, gleam at jobs, raise kids.

All too bloody likely accidentally colluding in a taboo that says we shouldn't talk about our periods or our menopause because we're nice girls. Heroines.

Except, excuse us, we're half the world, us women, more, and we've nothing to taboo about.

That includes those of us who couldn't bleed, because we were born in the wrong bodies, or didn't want to bleed, for the same reason, and had decisions made over our heads, which side-lined us even from ourselves.

Those of us whose bodies posed different challenges, which made us wish we could share the whole messy business after all.

Before we knew it, we and our fellow poets had created a place to shout, yell, rant, rave, laugh – like drains – and cry. So many, too, and a curse it was indeed to have to sift though all the contributions and choose between them.

To everyone who made it into the book, a big soppy thank you. And to all those who didn't, a teary wave: if we coulda we woulda welcomed you all in. We didn't because editing that many poems would really have sent us rushing for our hand-held, motorised windmills.

Next up: how should we order the book? We had quite a few clever ideas over the red wine, but luckily came to our senses over a nice cup of herbal tea. And opted for alphabetical by first name. More or less. Radical or what?

Well, ok, but fair at least. Only surprise, surprise: we found that there is a strange and stirring synchronicity in the way things have worked out.

We hope you'll enjoy (well, you know what we mean) the result. So go on, put your feet up. It's about bleeding time.

Gill Lambert And Rebecca Bilkau

While Bleeding

In a vintage boutique on Sullivan's Quay,
I lift a winter coat
with narrow bodice, neat lapels, tight waist, a fallen hem.
It is far too expensive for me,
but the handwritten label
[1915]
brings it to my chest in armfuls of red.

In that year, someone drew a blade
through a bolt of fabric
and stitched this coat
into being. I carry it
to the dressing room, slip my arms in;
silk lining spills against my skin.
I clasp the belt and draw a slow breath
as a cramp curls again
where blood stirs and melts.
In glass, I am wrapped in old red –

red pinched into girl cheeks,
and smeared from torn knees,
lipstick blotted in tissue, the scarlet
concealed in pale sheets – all the red
bled into pads and rags,
the weight of red, the wait for red
that we share.

In the mirror, the old coat blushes.

This pocket may once have sheltered something
precious: a necklace, a love letter, or
a fresh egg, feather-warm, its shell brittle
around a hidden inner glow, held loosely
so it couldn't crack, couldn't leak through seams,
so it couldn't stain the dress within.

Doireann Ní Ghríofa

Prince, You're Not My Saviour

King-daddy banned spindles when he heard the spell:
In her fifteenth year, Rose shall prick herself,
too tiny a corpse to show off.

It was a flax-ranch on the run
where I bumped into a spinning witch.
One swirl was enough, I fainted asleep,
all around blushing silence.
Eagles dropped their supper,
the meat stopped cooking in Death's pan.
Hedges were snoring away lad after lad.

Not you.

You brought me crippling news (you think).

Prince, you're witness of my fatherless pride.
I skip without my keeper, my captor.

Once sleeping beauty, I wake ripe.
What I exhale keeps away tepid rules.

Your finger ain't bled, not yet,
you stroke my snaky-fence curls
– thorn is a thorn is a thorn –
into the shape of a crown.

Agnes Marton

Rischio Di Tamponamento!

A traffic warning. Risk of pile-ups. Every time,
it tickles me. I imagine giant tampons,
round-nosed, gracefully ominous
barrage balloons, massing in a red sky
over Florence or Rome.

Takes me back to the shame
of a teenage party. My best friend
Mary, ahead of me in all ways,
got flowered bell-bottoms, a pony
and The Curse for birthday presents,

celebrated by draping the garage
(where *Michelle, ma belle* was in the air
and snogging was planned)
with strawberry nets. Strewn inside them,
the usual glass balls and buoys

and fleets of unwrapped Tampax, rafts
of loopy Doctor Whites, bullet-showers
of Lil-lets. An armoury for girls in the know,
a taunting *tamponamento*: pains and pitfalls,
secret remedies. I joined the festa,
hid my baffled questions, too risky to ask.

Alex Josephy

Cadences

Her first blood was rust brown, the size of an old 10p coin –
not what she expected. There was no time for celebration,
it was a fickle guest who left for a year and went
on a tour of all her friends first, before skulking back after dark.

Her second blood was a carmine tide,
unexpected, overnight – when shifting balances
messed with her head, and made her go to bed
wearing long johns and a fine woollen sweater.

There was no ceremony. Just a white wedge of help,
stuffed into a school bag, ridden all day, an uncomfortable horse,
whose brutal bulk would not hide inside her PE leotard.
It was a generous gift that could not, would not, be contained.

So it goes on.

The ebb and flow. The too much that was disbelieved
by white coated men, that could gather in goblets on a strange altar.
The time it stopped for three moons, then returned with a force
to release a child who wasn't ready or able to be in the same world.
The storm surges after three births that opened her like waterfalls.

The flow and ebb. The years of nursing and never knowing.
The flush and flood, a harmonic constitution of moon and sun.
Now an occasional lag in the pattern, liked dropped stitches
that range into lace and cast off. No longer residual as the
moon rests in a velvet case, and her bones begin to gleam.

Ali Jones

Menses

I bleed, and from my body
flows a stream
uniting me with all that's
fruitful in the earth.

I swell, and celebrate
the ripening corn, the apple
and the yeast which multiplies
the cells, sustaining life.

I feel
the rhythm of the tides
which rise and fall and draw
all waters to the sea.

And deep within my body
a lake reflects the glow that lights the night,
mirroring the moon,
pure centre of the rhythm that I share.

Alwyn Marriage

First published in Acumen and Touching Earth

The Supposed To Be Girl

A baby's tiny, mittened hands
Tied with pretty ribbons to metal crib bars.
Stopping her scratching scarlet itches,
A line of blue stitches,
Slashed above her groin.

She shouldn't have been born.
The assembly plan was not followed,
Was mixed up with another.
A supposed-to-be girl who didn't turn out the way
She was meant to.

Surgeons stitched over Nature's mistake;
Cutting out, slicing off, excising anything female and leaving
… nothing.
A baby girl who wouldn't grow up to be a woman.
Intersexed, no-sexed, a sterile cul-de-sac.

As her friends passed through puberty
To their womanhood beyond,
She was left behind.
And no amount of testosterone from a syringe
Could push her into a masculine world instead.

So as my friends bled normally,
I bled from bladed arms and wrists.
A bloody offering to the Goddess,
That she might receive me as her daughter
And make me whole.

I will be fifty-six next week.
The should-be me would be exploring life post-menopausal.
Instead I embrace a new puberty
As HRT suckles oestrogen-starved synapses, reforming my body,
Turning me at last into the girl I was supposed to be.

Angela Serena Gilmour

Special Permission At St Cuthbert's Primary

Sophie raises her hand and asks to be excused.
Mr Walker glances at the clock. It is two minutes
till break time, but he nods anyway.
As she closes the door behind her,
shrinking into the corridor's shadows,
Sophie hears one of the Harrison twins complaining
That's not fair, Sir and Mr Walker's calm voice
replying *Life's not fair, Gail.*

The secretary is not in her office.
A small fold of card on the counter says
Back in Five Minutes. Sophie frowns.
Sweat breaks out on her palms as she knocks
on the headteacher's door.
May I use the toilet? she asks.
Mrs Dunning offers her the key
and a sympathetic smile.

In the staff restroom the bag of towels
is stashed under the sink. They smell
vaguely of bleach and pot pourri.
They are Waitrose Own Brand, much softer
than the ones her mum buys at Priceright.
She slips a spare into her pocket;
she will use it when she goes to bed.
Already she has learnt that the price of economy
is poor absorbency and leakage.

By the time Sophie returns the key
her class has spilled out into the yard.
She turns away from the voices,
avoids the taunts of the twins:
We know where you've been to!
She selects a book from the library shelf,
leans against the radiator, allows
the warmth to flood through her.

Angi Holden

First Blood

I am maybe five
when I barge into the bathroom
questions forming
to find you afloat in a pool of crimson
shock of ink red liquid
white round body, belly, blood, white tub.
I fear you've cut yourself
are hurt

this happens to a woman
you explain.
You use the proper terms
vagina and lining and womb,
do not mention pain
or clots the size of fists
or the shame we sit in
all our lives.
The darkening stain of us
on the scrubbed white world.

Anna Cole

Perimenopause Of Trojan Proportion

Everywhere I go
    I am followed
        by a Greek Chorus.
Blank-eyed, aghast-mouthed,
    they wring their hands and call
I'm not well, not well, not well.

They speak an ancient language
    that nobody else – not my doctor,
    my partner, my child – can understand.
Perhaps their white masks are cells.
Perhaps their red gowns are bloods.
    Don't ask me.
Everything I don't know is legion
    and floods from me
and their mouths are
    many, many, many.

15 years back, I was singular.
I watched that Greek Chorus
    perform in *Women of Troy.*
I sat safely
    on the side of the audience.
Hot summer, I was newly in love
    and the horror onstage
did not really touch me
    but the red velvet seat
scratched my bare legs. A pinprick heart
beat in my womb,
    a new heroine
for an old, old, old story.

Anna Kisby

When My Fifties Came Stalking Like A Stray Cat

My kids left home at the same time   the worst that happened
was this hollowing out   I pictured my body as a dry husk

food stacked up in the fridge   milk soured and mould
claimed
                         the softness of cheese

My car limped along   with a dodgy clutch
                                    and worn out tyre-treads

My bed was unmade   each evening shuttered down
far too quickly   like a parade of bargain-
basement shops

Work piled up   on the tabletop
essays to mark   a manuscript half-cocked

                                    spreadsheets glaring
from the pale-blue glimmer of a laptop screen

I found myself frowning   for no apparent reason
                                    flicking the kettle switch

                 waiting for a boiling point
that came each evening and left me drenched   in sweat

the menopause-cat stayed   became sweeter in nature
                         less prone to yowling at the night

Anne Caldwell

Bloodline

You are the first to know.
I come to find you
whisper quietly to you
blood drying dark on the tips of my fingers
as though I have touched a sin.
You take me into our sunlit bathroom
press a pad into my hand
tell me to wash and then change my pants.
Leave me to my new ritual of clumsy silence and fresh new blood.

Later I walk downstairs for lunch;
feel the bulk of my new womanhood between my legs.
I glimpse your face.
Know, somehow, that a connection
to some dark unravelling has begun.

You are long gone before I cease to bleed.
Years later, I will come to understand
with a new and piercing sense of loss
that the timeline of my menstruation has disappeared with you.
I cannot claim my inheritance.
My bloodline.
This journey I will take alone.

Anne McMaster

Follow The Scent

A girl is born, grows up and bleeds.
Once a month, give or take

a day or two, she curls up on herself
and cradles the stain that fits

in her hand: one spot, enough to form
a wormhole to a realm that's hers alone.

For this girl bleeds and refuses to meet
the expectations thrown at her.

There will be no children:
even her dolls were never babies.

The olfactory trail left by the blood
no longer wanted by her body

leads her down beneath the flow
to the place where she laments

the loss of a furry tail she never had,
a pelt handed down the fairy tales,

yet the call to reinvention remains
unanswered for want of permission.

B. Anne Adriaens

Black Mensa Landscape

You write about my flower as if I think and see what you
think and see of it – and I don't.

Georgia O'Keefe

The sun of my primordial follicle
rises over layered landscape. Undulating folds
fill the frame, leave a shard of snow-cap, a sliver of sky.
Coral hills beckon, hems sprouting trees of prehistoric green;
beyond, blue-black mountains hold their truth firm.

The eye can see music: to see takes time.
When your eye sees, that sun has squeezed through
died its death. A second emerges, every month a new progress,
each repeating the first act at menarche.

Dare you shoot into the blue – an arrow may pierce a sun,
peel a half light for months, before the sequence rolls again,
over and over, until the last sun spent, the scenery dims.

I bloomed to make you see; you thought you knew
all about me. In me more lives are buried, than you can ever dream.

Barsa Ray

O'Keefe painted varied subjects: flowers, New York skyscrapers and landscapes. Black Mesa
Landscape is one of her works on her beloved New Mexico.

Reduced Ovarian Reserve

The mountain appeared overnight on the 1st September 1730.
The earth had been shouting for days.
People knew then to listen to her warnings
so the Majo sailed off for the mainland.

After Timanfaya I thought my dreams, so often barren,
would be angry with lava, its blackened remains;
instead they were laden with a woman's most ordinary loss.
The mountain appeared overnight on the 1st September 1730.

For six years, night skies were spurted with blood,
smoke carried. A priest recorded it in his notes
as though God's witness to the apocalypse;
the earth had been shouting for days.

There were new fissures weekly and caves opening like vulvas.
The priest did not write of their kinship to vulvas
but fertility symbols of the island were prescient;
people knew then to listen when the earth gave her warnings.

They tried to make sense of the destruction; from the lava
discerned veins and lips, the muscularity of limbs,
tried to find hope's patterns in the wind-blown sand. Failed.
So the Majo sailed off for the mainland.

Hilario stayed and planted a fig tree. It took root
but didn't fruit because of the heat. We can't always ensure
what is sown can reach its potential.
The mountain appeared overnight.

Becky Cherriman

Unregulated

Only at the end of our story
did our clockwork begin to sync.
Which went to prove my gyny's theory
of how polycystic ovaries think.

But once that last drop was bled
upon the pristine white bed sheet
did I feel what long wanted to be said
about my wayward bleeds, the evasive baby feat

that I had failed at so often and epically,
leaving me feeling alien, other, strange
in the company of women who monthly
bitched, moaned, rejoiced, baned.

Post-menopausal I was back inside the fold
where both the maidens and the crones do not bleed.
I am again a regular woman, never again to be told
that I am pathological for lacking a regular bleed

in the usual rhythms of most female lives.
I am now again on the same woman level
holding power within my sacred hive
that finds new vigour and is ever heedful.

Bee Smith

The Curse

It's not ladylike to swear.
Well, fuck that, fuck this and fuck you.
There's no lady present
when I'm on my knees washing bloody-black clumps
from my favourite knickers, the sheets, the towels:
weeping in pain and fury and relief
at another lucky escape.

Swilling down painkillers with cheap beer
and leftover gateaux. Black Forest, with sour red cherries,
squishing through my fingers and provoking
memories of the days before this agony of woman:
handbag-free walks, unkissed lips,
dancing no matter who was watching.

But at least the sickening migraine is gone now,
the tender boobs,
the heart attack in my womb,
the bloating and the aching and the cramping,
the checking every chair when I stand up.
The secrecy of the curse incanted every month.

Twenty-eight fucking days and counting.

Bev Morris

Consultation

The only difference you'll notice
is that you will have lost
your fertility and you won't have periods

but you've proved your fertility
and who'd want to have periods?
Me. I would. I must be weird.

But then I stopped ovulating
and he said *That's what happens,*
your ovary just gives up

but it won't age you. You won't
go through an early menopause
And then I did and I plucked out grey hairs

and I tried every diet, spent a fortune
on moisturiser, did my roots
with a toothbrush,

washed drenched sheets,
wore low necks for fear of hot flushes
in front of year eleven bottom set,

flung open windows in winter,
ran into the cool garden,
took the horse piss pills

became someone else.
Bloody hell you don't look it,
that's something to be proud of.

And I was. I liked not looking it,
I was like that woman in Dickens
who had so many spare parts

when she died they found nothing
just a heap of dust in the bed,
a false leg, dentures and a wig.

Carole Bromley

Advice From The Afterlife About Periods

And this is what she said, in a voice like grass:
when your monthly visitor comes calling,
swishing her scarlet cloak, make her welcome
even though she'll have the muscles of a titan
and the gob of a fishwife. If you're unlucky
she'll poke a pole in your belly and stir it around.
Don't sob too loudly when you count up the months
you'll bleed in your life time. Never leave
the scarlet blossom of a clot in the toilet bowl:
men might see it. Don't complain if your thighs
get chafed when you insist on going horse riding
with that big, bloody slug between your legs.
Know that you'll smell like the butcher's shop
on Clarendon Street if you don't keep yourself clean.
Eat a plate of liver and bacon, shiny with gravy.
Think yourself lucky. It will pass. Too soon, it will pass.

Caroline Gilfillan

Loss

The blood was the balm, my kiss;
holding on like red anemones. Cocoon.
Keep warm and burrow, little rabbit.
Hot soil cups the sun's every curve –
balance the little ball.

But the grip goes. She's gone, and
night-dark drops to swallow the light.
She's old iron, in my hands, alone,
both in pieces, like rose petals
dying.

Caroline Hardaker

Wherefore Art Thou Crinoline Lady?

Didst thou, dear lady, hide 'neath thy skirts
Most voluminous, a bucket? To catch thy
Red Flow? To sitteth upon in quiet corners
And groan? Didst grip a hottie to thy stomacher?

Thy waist, dear lady, was such that thou surely
Hadst no internal organs for t'was miniscule.
Was thine inner self crushéd by whalebones
And corsetry lacings most vicious?

Pray, dear lady, didst thou have a Great Bloody
Stain sopping the arse of thy crinolines for
We never didst see thee walketh away
But rather coy, a trifle sideways didst thou sidle.

Didst thy bonnet hide thy bilious visage?
For lo, thine exalted place is took dear lady
By *DISPOSAL BAG* with brutish clear instructions.
Hast thou retiréd to the Land of Hot Flushes?

Char March

Reunion

The Spain I remember is twenty six years away
when I wore youth carelessly
in that pension in the old town
mercifully dark and cool,
where a cello echoed daily,
and I was long limbed and didn't notice
what trace I left in the world.

I do now, when my impact
is more often than not invisible
I have brought in my suitcase
all the baggage of this age
but the airport scanners are not
programmed to detect menopause.
This city echoes me, its central river dammed
because preservation is a necessary response
to arid months, the lifeblood
now gone to grass, moss and mud,
graffiti and a stench of drains.

Yesterday we took the train to Carminito Del Rey,
clung to wooden walkways 100m above a river gorge.
I have been clinging for some time now.

I leave a trail of husks, a litter of unfinished poems
their little skins too shrivelled to hold fruit,
their carcasses picked clean of flesh,
we are dried out with nothing left.

I see myself twenty six years back in a halter neck,
walking to a taverna for sangria and tapas.

I'm still here, I'm still here.
The sun will blossom me again –
for myself this time.

Charlotte Ansell

♪ The Elephant Song

Early   warning   signs   of   stress
   Sudden   weight   loss   or   weight   gain
   Tired   but   can't   sleep   excessive   fatigue
      Speech   difficulties   impatience
  Headaches   repeated   colds   or   flu
    Nail   biting   teeth   grinding
   Low   or   high   blood   sugar
   Low   or   high   blood   pressure
   High   cholesterol   or   triglycerides
    Ulcers   and   gastric   disturbances
   Chest   pains   muscle   aches
  Lower   back   shoulder   neck   pain
   Menstrual   problems   hair   loss
Forgetfulness

                      *

Forgetfulness
        loss   weight   gain
loss
            head   signs
ache
          problems   problems
            pain
            neck
          shoulder
            back
           chest

Early   warning   signs   of   memory

                  *

                                  eth lethe nap gons ♪

Chaucer Cameron

found poem from web list for signs of stress – & PMDD

22

The First Felt Lucky

The first felt lucky: I had been waiting.
Breasts would follow, the pluck I was certain hid
like a diamond in the slurry of my shyness.
A year of it and I was sick. I had waited
so long to be a woman. Had expected beauty
to settle on me. Beauty and calm.
Instead it was clubbed stomachs, catcalls from scaffolds.
Never my stepfather's hands but his eyes.
I wanted to take it all back. The blood I scrubbed
from cooled stripes to clear water.
The cramps that worked me like knuckled dough.
I didn't want to be marked out
as a room for men to spend the night. Where life could root,
or infection. I wanted to be pure and clear
as chapel glass, for light to pass
right through me.
For years, I lived on mints and water. Fell in love
with hunger. My sky was the size of a hospital window,
my waist a zero of finger and thumb.
My underwear was impossibly white.
The second time I bled for the first time, I cried
for the life that was over. Now I was back
to wet metals on the cotton tongue
of my knickers, water-bottles cuddled cold.
Dress sizes climbing from single figures to two.
I creaked like an old ship as I grew into air I'd vacated,
leaking rust like an old radiator.
If I knew then what I know now, I'd have given thanks
to the moon.
But how could I have imagined it.
Wine in the bathtub, wheels of cheese.
The man I love
drawing a gentle fingertip over my belly,
like a surgeon closing a wound.

Cheryl Pearson

Nine Lines

bucket-soaking sheets
sopping pads wrapped chip-shop tight
nightly burning shame

blood-flushed last chance child
empty useless barren womb
monthly bleeding shame

fear-filled muck-sweat nights
raging alien cuff-snagged brain
end this bloody shame

Chris Grogan

Climate Change

In the toilet cubicle of a café I inspect my knickers for threads of stale brown blood. I am losing my eggs. My body is coiled and doesn't wrap them in tissue so I can mourn them. They slip out unnoticed. I don't think I have many eggs left. Some days I shriek for them, perhaps on a day when one emerges. Maybe it sits in the lining of my knickers. Or I flush it away with wipe of recycled toilet roll. Yoke less.

My children have developed a taste for eggs. We turn them into birthday cakes and forget to put shells into the compost. We put candles on the transformed eggs and blow them out with hip hip hoorays.

My body is preparing for a great ceremony of grieving. My skin dries and wrinkles. Grey hairs twist out of hair dye, insistent. The world is broiling. My eight year old daughter cries herself to sleep because sea turtles eat plastic bags believing they are jelly fish. I cry because of my eggs. And my hatchlings.

Christina Wilson

The Menses

Curling at the edges, my flower
heads glow in the late sun,
my fragrance is faint.

Once, I stretched my stem, straining
to burst my buds, releasing,
at last, the mossy soft petals.
Plump, succulent, open,
they were soothed by morning air.
My stamens, heavy with pollen,
trembled for the bee's intimacy,
the tiny vibrations of translucent wings.
Languidly, my leaves leaned their long
fingers into luscious foliage.
As the sun warmed, my sickly sweetness
mixed with the scent of flowers close by,
making an invisible mist of vivid red.
Tugged inwards, I drained down
to my roots, where, deep in soil,
my sticky nectar flowed.

Now, I am relaxed, full blown,
sashaying gently in the soft breeze,
content to be on my own, undisturbed.

Clare Wigzell

Growing Wrong

They never gave me the words, for fear of teaching me
how to be all the nightmares a parent doesn't want their child to be.
I was born only to find as I grew my body betrayed me,
becoming a cancer growing parts that were surely not meant for me.
Met with suspicious eyes over dinner night after night,
I hid new words acquired by black market trading,
longing to learn the language to aid me.
But my body bleeds oceans of red month after month,
I can't part myself from its hex; change the rage I feel,
deal with the smug looks of this is the way things should be,
what is this slow agonising grief?
To spot blood, pay for aids to conceal and contain,
to hate myself for giving me away, guilt, shame.
Pay then display, my words mimed: *I am male, I am male.*
Words found and lost in a society that states:
you were born this way, your paperwork says.

Dalton Harrison

Red

I gaze into the mirror and I see the future in my face.
It forms with every line the past has left behind.
I feel the wheel of change inside. It churns and turns full circle.

As I button up to brave the cold, I smile at the colour of my coat.
For I have been Red Riding Hood,
my crimson cloak, a flag, a warning, an invitation.
I have seen the wolf, his nostrils flared at the scent of my flowing blood.
I have heard his bated breath, just close enough to pounce.

I have carried secrets with me through the woods.
I have given them away.
I have felt afraid, excited, all dressed up in women's clothes.
I've climbed into a bed that wasn't mine and satisfied my hunger.
For girls can be wolves too.
I have laid as still as stone, while a man has cut my aching, bulging, belly open,
and pulled out a screaming child.

I gaze into the mirror and I see the future.
A face, the colour of the moon that no longer stirs me, but guides me on,
reminds me where the path was always leading. To grandma's house.
Is she who I'll become? A grey old lady who sits and waits,
for the grace of grandchildren, for the kindness of handsome strangers,
my only company the trees and sky?
Must I wait for this final visitor, to knock on my door, to gobble me up?

Perhaps. But for now, I have big eyes, and teeth, my blood still runs.
I'll wear my crimson cloak, my flag, my warning, my invitation.
And I'll keep my secrets.

Daniela Nunnari

How Change Comes – *and not in a good way*

So there you are in a kind of semi-continuous sunshine in which all things are alive and benevolent. And then the first blow – not only are they not all benevolent but they are not all alive, and worse – if they are alive, they will die and so will you. Not good, but never mind – you recover, sort of.

One morning, you wake up as an astronaut, way out in space (but safe, always safe), the next day, you strut your stuff on stage – a bit Shakespeare, a bit Lady Gaga. At this point in your life, it's much the same, and you can switch between roles so easily. Explorer, inventor – the name is less important than the game you play each day that opens up your world. And then they drop new horrors into your life.

If you're a girl, then you will bleed. No reason is given, just – *well, you're growing up, isn't that good? It happens. Deal with it.* No discussion. *Oh yes, and you'll need some of these. Let me know when.* And then they go about their day. No more to say.

As your body changes, so does your sense of self in space and time. Some of the delight you knew is shrinking, pulling back from possibilities, and words become, perhaps, of more importance than the act of being new for real, because real is constricting and full of expectations placed on you. There is suddenly a gap, a chasm, between self and other ways to be. It all shuts down, and there you are, a very different kind of me.

Hope you can deal with it.

Denni Turp

Mr Gie Does Some Lovely Work

Ten years gone and you're not missed,
I've almost forgotten what you did.
Getting my innards in such a twist,
it was so much easier to just be rid.
My quick decision to cut you loose
was abrupt blessing in bruised disguise;
no need to tolerate more abuse,
being together never had any highs.

I didn't need you in the first place,
so simple then to say a swift farewell.
Now all that's left of you is one trace
invisible to all, that only I can tell:
engraved forever, without guile,
below bikini line – my six-inch smile.

Di Slaney

Blood-Dimmed

The blood-dimmed tide is loosed,
and everywhere the ceremony of innocence is drowned
                    Yeats, The Second Coming

We read each other that poem, you know the one?
The one about the worst being full of passionate intensity,
the one about slouching to Bethlehem to be born.
With you I felt rebirthed, just as I was croning. That time
                              and tides didn't matter.

You charted my heats and chills, pronounced that your 'pause
would be the same. The way of wild women, you said.
Free of synthetic clothes, hormones, mores.
Oblivious to any other way I basked in your approval.
It went on like that for years:

Me sanguine, you bloodier.
Did I mention we read each other that poem?
The world got wilder, more untamed, cast off its own mores.
I couldn't aquaplane on slicks of blood with you but it was passionate, still.
No lack of love or conviction. And then you left.

For someone bloodier, prone to icy dips and hot sessions, full of
passionate intensity. Part of what felt like a blood tide
That would spare no-one. The shore, the tide, the breakers would bleed.
Another wave of feminism happened and women talked
                              of coming together.

Cooler blooded, crouched on the shore, I was no longer sure.
The blood between women is not always bright.

Elizabeth Carola

Luxury Alice

Alice pushed the duster into tight green corners.
Even when times had been tough
she'd refused to sell,
content to starve among
their cottony comfort.
Everyone, she believed,
deserved a little luxury.
Some women opted for Italian handbags,
Alice remained devoted to women's sanitation.

Two vintage display cabinets held most of her collection –
top shelves reserved for those with wings,
bottom shelves for the 'heavy flow' editions.
A line of fluffy white mice with string tails
posed on the mantelpiece,
spotlights enhanced sleek white curves of liners
whose sticky backs were plastered
along the feature wall.

It was worth the expense,
the additional taxes,
for moments like this –
she squeezed one pudgy green packet,
knowing that they were hers. Always.

Emilie Lauren Jones

Paula Dunn

A Second Attempt With The Menstrual Cup

Slippery with blood
warm in my fingers
the resistant cup
wriggled
nudged
propelled by my grip
disappeared back up

Bearing down it emerged
reluctant at first
then goldfish slippery it leapt from my hand
a failed catch
incompetent snatch
a bloody shipwreck
sunken in the pan

Dredged from the depths
medical grade silicone
tarnished with shit
again
mummified cup
stuffed in a pocket
unsuspecting pants heavily wadded.

Emily Reynolds

Gold

Arched back and frantic shoulders.
Grinding hands,
fabric against fabric,
ringing misted droplets of fire from dampened cotton.

And you watch in fear
as crimson flirts with bath water,
teasing out that final watermark of *shame*.

Shame
should the male gaze fall upon your *embarrassment*.
The *stain* of your essence.

Shame
should the ebb and flow of your body remind him
that Mother Nature's bloodied teeth lie between your thighs
instead of his dominance.

Shame
that the warmth which brought the flush of sex to your cheek
now brings scorn
a curling lip
a not-so-hidden grimace.

A shame
that the power which runs through your veins
and through the veins of his mother
could be treated as *poison*.
That gilded strength,
that treasured femininity,
that falling fruit, ripened into blood orange
and goldenberry.

Emily Rose

The First Time

Here's me held hostage by the sand
as other kids splashed and swam.

Here's me wondering if you can see
this pad – the size of a lilo

or a 2 man dinghy. Here's me
trying to out-scream the gulls.

Me holding a simmering competition
with the sun. Me squally

face hidden, hunched and furious
over a rock pool. Watching

clots of anemones, shift easily
between one state and another.

Emma Purshouse

Climacteric Forecast

Storm warning:
low pressure belly,
cyclonic guts,
high pressure breasts.

Bouts of depression
with squally moods expected.
Fog on the brain,
may clear later.

Risk of flash floods
in some areas.
High humidity predicted
overnight.

Possible improvement by the weekend,
with a few bright spells
as ovulation front
moves south.

Long term outlook:
unsettled periods
decreasing in frequency
with higher temperatures than expected.

Patches of HRT may bring some sunny intervals.

Emma Storr

After The Hysterectomy

This must be confusing
states my cousin
I mean   radical your ovaries
fallopian tubes
womb   gone

Yes I am confused
This bleeding   rip shredding
flood blooding   teeth clamped
clenching   tissue tearing
defines me?

Womb equals woman
woman equals womb?
Oxymorons
silent scream   open secret
cars with no engines
beached boats with torn sails
emus ostriches penguins

Those scarlet tsunamis
raging rivers of red   gone
now I am teacher gardener cook
friend lover
Me

Finola Scott

Unravelling

Who is this whispering in my head?
   Cut the grass and pick the peas
   Dry the comfrey, chip the rosemary
   The peppers need water and look how the brambles reach

I have dropped the secateurs under the apple tree
unreachable below nettle and thorn
gloves, stupid! – Take the job seriously.

My mind is weed-riven like the terraces,
brambled and webbed with sticky burrs
hidden under the sudden army of balsam
mean nettles and the smoky heads of Rosebay

I creep forward into my mental plot,
meaning to gather a crop of creativity
but driven back, stung and scratched,
tripped by old roots and barred by wild growth.

Ideas I watered in the deep of night
are frail laced leaves, feeding the caterpillars,
and the black seeds from the Himalayas uncoil
spraying my fears all over the fertile earth.

Freda Davis

In Tune

We wear our hearts on our tongues
and our mouths are full of heavy rhythms.

Our corridors are fuggy and warm
with the scent of rusty iron,
drift-tide and brewers yeast.

Our loyal cats keep their claws sharp
and we ache and stain as the days
scoop out our unused meat,
leave molehills of dark, jammy flesh
quivering in our bathrooms.

We swear more than usual.
We feel more than usual.
We see more than usual.
The air around us is clear, sharp braille
that our fingers read with ease.
We can hear what you're thinking.

Every clock in our weeping mansion
bleeds in sympathy
knowing more than any of us
about time.

Gaia Holmes

Painting-By-Numbers
for H

I have never been able to draw.
At school two girls who were good at it
showed me how by following the lines
with your eyes while you make
the same marks with your pencil on paper.

My dad once helped me paint-by-numbers;
tiny spaces filled in with weird-named oils.
Forests in Alpine, ten shades of green,
the relief of blue for a mountain stream.

It was painted on plastic then shrunk
in the oven so it looked for all the world
like a miniature masterpiece.
I think he framed it.

I can't draw. But there are things I can tell you:
how you can alter the image
you have of yourself, rub out the lines,
take yourself to bits piece by piece.
Build yourself up again.

And though you look different: you are
a tango dancer in Buenos Aires,
a grandmother, long-distance swimmer,
you *are* still the same.

And one day there is no more paint,
no more pieces, you've filled all the spaces
with different colours. It's beautiful;
you can hardly believe you have made it.
I think you should frame it.

Gill Lambert

Nothing To Wear

It's the weekend and you've nothing to wear.
Mum has no suggestions,

so the loo roll keeps on giving
until its depletion attracts attention.

The chemist accepts pocket money as currency.
Sanitary booty is smuggled home

a small bump of phantom pregnancy –
teenage shame greater than a bleed.

Gillian Mellor

She Said Birth

could irreparably damage my body,
and wouldn't advise children.
I leave the appointment with contraception –
bleed for a whole month, tampons binned
like reminder letters. I find I rest my hand
against my stoma bag – firm and warm
like a baby bump. This body is pregnant
with the unknown; its nerves spent matches
which smoulder. Each month, this body prepares
for a party it can never hold.

Hannah Hodgson

Blood Sister

She is twenty, barely old enough to be on adult oncology.
She has dad's hazel eyes, mum's prominent nose.
When we were kids we were lumped together
as 'the girls' in between 'the boys.'
When the bathroom bin filled with bloodstained waste,
mum would give each of us a creepy hug,
running her hands down our bums to feel
the telltale bulge of sanitary towel,
checking which of her daughters was performing as planned.
My sister was the clever one, good at science.
When she went to med school the space opened up
for us to become close.

She is twenty, I am nineteen. She has the lopsided smile
of a person diagnosed (wrongly) with Bell's Palsy.
No-one will admit she is dying.
My mother praises the Lord at Easter
for a resurrection lifting of symptoms
(in fact, it's steroids faking it).
I perch on her hospital bed.
We have our first and last conversation about the curse.
'You know,' she slurs, through paralysed lips,
'it's one thing to wonder if your period is going to come,
another to wonder if you'll ever have one again.'
She never bled again. Me, every twenty-five days like clockwork,
and years after my fibroid-engorged uterus
was 'whipped out' in protracted surgery,
I still bleed for her.

Hannah Stone

Curse

The goddess bled into the earth
and babies formed
congealed and glorious
like fleshy fruit.

And life went on like this
with beads and lunar counting
until the wild dogs hit
with their beastly appetites.

Hence, girls were strung up in cages
when they waxed unclean,
lest milk turn to vinegar
or sea lay siege to fishermen.

And now the goddess,
thin as a whistle
hugs the hospital blanket
to her waning self.

Each glaring day on the ward
she makes a shiv from the moon
and cuts a tidy red line
into the narrow rise of her belly.

Helen Ivory

First published in The Atomical Venus *Bloodaxe*

Bloodless Beauty

My first show was at school, Spring term.
Back home, they remember me always
in cheap green crop top and too tight
size 10 second-hand Armani jeans,
strutting the stuff. 'A natural!' they said.
Like the stain I found later on my pants.
'Decorators in!' Painting my puberty and
rouge-blushing my chiselled cheekbones.

Still a teen, when my Summer season came,
signed up to London catwalks, where real
money and men were to be had. Size 6 gets
you sex that sells, in bed and in the papers.
Model/party-girl, labelled and made-over.
Injected against the monthly 'curse' (used
to needles by now). Learning to be dry
and bloodless. Frees you for more work.

Autumn, I'd hoped would be Paris,
mellow in 'haut' with Yves and Coco.
Magazine work instead. Leather back in,
with chic hints of S&M in cruel-heeled boots.
Thinning out my life, dwindling as they want,
so no flesh can get in way of the clothes.
Sometimes working tables to get by –
roulette until luck ran out, then the cafs.

No need now for injections, when you don't eat.
The white line man brings all I need. Snow
for Winter season. My 'change' has come too soon.
Fertility sacrificed for their emaciated 'femininity'.
Less of a woman is always more. Fashionably pale,
I long for the old moon to tug my belly back to life,
make it swell and sluice with woman's nurturing blood.
But can only stare at the phone, waiting the next call.

Helen Shay

Hysterectomy Blues

Cry, cry, cry, woman.
Cry for the scarring,
the missing, the past.

Cry for the nerves,
for their undelivered messages.

Cry when he comes to you,
cry when you hold your children.

Cry, cry, cry, woman,
hold your stitches and cry.

Cry for the flowers he doesn't bring,
cry for the hours he spends working,
cry for that thing you can't name.

Cry, cry, cry, woman.
Cry for him slow dancing
at the office party.

Cry for the only clue,
cry for that.
Cry, cry, cry.

Hilary Robinson

Witch Club

At the ready, sisters!
Daub period blood like war-stripes
Over all mischievous faces. TAKE. UP. SPACE.
Spread your legs wide and come inside.
A place to banish shame, shake cosmic ass,
Sing songs about the potency of pussy
And of course – take time out,
To meditate upon the earth as mother.
Make mushroom brews on full moons
Nestled in the bosom of all your witchy women.
Suggest fake ritual dances, get *possessed*,
Bless a fire of polka dot coats and sequins, the odd glittery bag
And burn symbols of patriarchy like rags … their power long gone.
Then leave the pub, arm in arm and pissed,
Having ganged up on a perv and given him some shit,
And let it be therapeutic, and healing
As you walk home together, chanting
Witch Club. Witch Club. Witch Club.
Let's menstruate with the lunar cycle,
Create blood-red tides to tie our sistren together, forever.
We might only meet up once a month,
But when we do, we are *terrible*.
Currently, we are concentrating on casting
Binding spells on sociopathic world leaders,
Evicting nasty spirits, armed with only
A toy drum, a cunt and a smudge stick.
We are the patriarchy catchers.
Each month we grow more wolf-like and yes, a bit militant.
We are taken over by it, so fired up on unholy cuntmunion
(Otherwise known as feminism, but shhh, wouldn't wanna scare anyone).
At the ready, sisters!
Daub period blood like war-stripes
Over all mischievous faces.
Be lover, maiden, mother, queen, huntress, sage and mystic
All. At. Once. Here, you are free, you can *shapeshift*.
Welcome to WITCH CLUB WITCH CLUB WITCH CLUB WITCH
CLUB WITCH CLUB

Izzy Brittain

Cycle

And there's a certain drawing down & I'm a child
again, fascinated as my nan hooks the chimney's
tongue

to pull breath from outside, tall the fire taller.
The creature in me burrows deeper, gnaws as if
trying

to treasure my bones. I fever every layer of skin,
on turning leave a glistening trail like something in
peril.

There is nowhere I can be, tremble in the in-between
when stars are being blinded by a melodramatic
morning.

Seismic shifts curl me undone, river my youth,
the promise of it falling wordlessly, reaching to be
held.

J V Birch

First published in A Bellyful of Roses *Ginninderra Press*

Bloodsong

The beast inside is disinclined,
as years go by, to hold a tune,
to keep the peace or come on time.

It won't perform its usual tricks,
bend to the carrot or the stick
or heed the mandate of the moon.

O salted song of broken glass
O sea of rust, O breaking flood
O waves of pain that will not pass

inflicted by some violent god,
you want them gone, you learn to curse
the raucous tides that will not turn,

but turn they will, to sudden loss.
How strange to wake one bloodless dawn
to silence where there once was song.

As absence fills your mortal core,
still, bless the stillness, white and pure
that holds you, weeping, on the shore.

Jacqueline Saphra

Time Of The Fucking Month

Fuck
your liver and bacon, butcher's apron, pound of mince,
got the painters in bullshit.
Fuck
your ride the white pony, time of the month,
on the rag. Riding the crimson tide – what the
fuck?
Who the hell is Auntie Flow and why is she surfing a Red Wave?
Up yours shark week. Lady Time – seriously? What a
fuck
ing load of tosh. These are not our Lady Days. Switch
the hell off that Red Light. We don't need to come with a warning.
Fuck
that. Run…Don't Walk! It's…The Blob. I thought it was IKEA
had Lingonberry Week. We are not Cursed. Mad Cow Disease?
Fuck
right off. Jam rag, jam rag – hey world, let's just call it
what it is. Menstruation is not a dirty word –
fuck
the euphemisms. They've been put there to make us ashamed.
I will not be putting Little White Mice anywhere up my cunt.
Fuck
during your bleed if you want to – this is not a disgusting thing.
Society has taught you to hide. Like it's something unnatural.
Fuck
sake, it's not. Unclean! Girl Flu. Birthing a blood diamond. Code Red,
let's shed the embarrassment of slang. Come on, lets call it what it is.
Period.

Jane Burn

Beneath

Angry older girls
rulers of St Mary's school
mob me in a cubicle
pressure me for proof
of playground claims
that my first period
despite my youth
had already come
my pants are dragged down
as I'm forced centre of a sorry stage
recasting them forever
slow for their age

Jane Campbell

If Men Had Periods.

If men had periods, we'd celebrate menarche
a triumphant rite of passage, back thumping
musical fanfares, cheered chants of joy.
welcoming our new addition to the tribe.

Red tents would be mandatory, serene
sanctuaries to take time out, do not
disturb, it's my bleed time, on digital
calendars, e-mail autoresponders.

Sanitary products would be celebrity
endorsed, sponsoring the Six Nations.
emblazoned on football pitches, Beckham
with his favourite brand of tampons.

Strava would chart ebb and flow,
monthly rhythms, lengths of cycle,
bleed intensity, compared via WhatsApp,
snapchat, discussed over a pint, or two.

Menopause would be the ultimate
accolade, wisdom well of knowledge,
tribal elder, well respected leader,
battle scars resplendent and admired.

We're not quite there yet, red
tide turning slowly, hormonal,
hysterical, feisty and frigid, labels
that will, one day, no longer stick.

Blood of our foremothers, grand
mothers, great grandmothers flows.
Our matrilineal line is strong, sisters,
daughters, nieces, neighbours keep the faith.

Our time will come.

Jen Hawkins

Palm Sunday

When they paved the hill it was perfect,
smooth all the way down. I had
my grandfather's skateboard. It was
dare or nothing.
And everything was
              hunky
                      dory
big lazy Ses
                  but
no-reason panic and I bailed onto
the Holmstedts' front yard –
not quite managing –
my hand scalded and scraped
and cradled home.

A bit of this, a bit of that,
a bandage, no time now, time for church.

All during Mass I colluded
with Christ. We spaced out.
We watched
blood above, blood below,
everything unclean about me
welling, bleeding through.

Jennifer A McGowan

A Blessing And A Curse

I had just turned seventeen.
Prayers to join my blooded sisters,
to be ripely plucked by Demeter,
were answered with a few brown stains.
Monthly torpor: the taste of iron,
dark gobbets preceding a week of pain
the relief of lost life spasms –
the joy of a still flat belly.

Then when I thought I would bleed
until each egg was released,
when each scarlet rag, instead of relief
brought the stab of loss: it stopped.
My daughter, born in my fortieth year
fulfilled Demeter's blessing.
As she grew this volatile, sensitive child
sucked energy from my life to hers.

Her hair curled, thickened to a blonde halo,
my silvered hair swirled down the plug.
The soapy smell of her skin as my raspberries
tickled her belly – fair reward for a saggy gut.
Teen and menopausal tempers collided.
My fevered skin, capricious moods:
her rage to be free, her need to be close.
We screamed and slammed our pain.

At last, when I thought I was free to grieve
for what might have been, to reclaim life
without Demeter's hormonal gifts,
my daughter began to bleed.
Sleepless nights returned –
she partied till dawn:
her mood an unpredictable whirlpool,
her love affairs bruising our hearts.

Then she was gone.

Jenny Robb

Blood-Letting

There are rubies twitching inside me, like sparkled suns they lurk,
he was proud to see the streaks left on the sheets,
we never talk about them now. He liked the blood's feel between
his fingers, liked the taste. *Must not waste the elixir*
he said. Now we sleep in separate beds, I hear him snore through
shut doors and our smells conjoin to make imaginary twins.
Take me back in, I cry, as the months get longer, and the cactus
on the shelf yearns to bloom. We never talk about those things.
I grab the thorns to get into my skin, to feel the noise of blood.

Jessica Mookherjee

The Visitor Who Ends Up Staying Forever

Embrace her like your grandmother,
the one who smelt of home,
cinnamon and sweat

She's here to stay, anklets tinkling,
petals shedding from her braids,
her full skirt swishing
against your wooden floor

Make her a cup of *chai*,
give her your favourite seat,
yes, that one by the window,
the one of the sunrise over the old oak tree,
and the visiting tits hungry for peanuts

In her are your ancestors, all
the women who came before
In her are your dreams
of unborn children

In her you are complete
and in her, you find your way home

Jhilmil Breckenridge

Crone

I saw her come in on a June tide,
silver and bone.
Met her on the ninth crest,
her white mare's breath
took salt and iron from me.
She left me with pearl, belladonna
and sand.

This Midwinter she gave me a crimson gift.
I bled out the worst of the year,
moved with the tides,
remembering salt and iron.

I saw her today as the sun lowered
and time breached a new decade.
She rose from slack tide
quieter, wreathed in blue light,
reached shore and we touched.

She is in me now.

Crescent moon rides the rim of space.
Belladonna flowers in my hand.

Josie Moon

Overwhelm

Her ovaries are articulate but that's the least of her worries; she is suffering from a yeast infection, and just this morning she shut her fingers in the door. Ovaries speak out loud of fertility, or at least of that monthly overwhelm for sex. It's tomorrow's red face and it's never pretty, but her head is, as they say, screwed on properly, she knows how not to give in to primitive desires. She has her book-learning and her crochet; she has the bowl of crocuses her mother gave her. Her mother always said *well at least you reproduced dear, but it was never going to be easy on your own.* Some days she wonders how many eggs are left, how many urges. She remembers unsuitable men she almost slept with, but tries not to dwell on it or she'd never get anything done.

Julia Webb

The First

a narrow house in a narrow street
a tight red room,
walls blackened with anger
a cold bath

a mean window in a mean town
a trembling hand
tears are running down the walls
a locked door

a tight ache in a tight belly
a forlorn hope
stains of shame in the morning
a blank wall

Julie Darling

Thought Forays

At night the ceiling deploys
all kinds of cooking utensils.
One scoops hot butter

on our griddle-bed. Others
prod and roll, back and forth.
By dawn my skin

is punctured
and hissing. All sides
are evenly scorched.

In the dark, I lob
thoughts like bricks
at neighbouring windows.

Wide-eyed and barred
from dreams, I upturn bins
that spill a past of scavenging.

Over breakfast, you say
you woke to the crunch
of slippers on broken glass.

We sip coffee
granules dissolving
rat corridors in charred grass.

Karen Hodgson Pryce

I Can Count Them On My Fingers

There were two before I got pregnant;
I didn't suspect I was. My girlfriend
bought a pregnancy test after
announcing, 'You've got tits!'
Positive explained the Twister Lolly
cravings, but not much else.

I'd seen the doctor once in eight
years – requesting amphetamines –
my notes read: 'Possible anorexic.
Amenorrhea.' Absence of menstrual
blood, lack of evidence, didn't
mean absence of mood swings.

I created a ritual to mark the event –
hennaed my hair each month –
tearfully, irritably, feeling a cheat.
It was almost a relief when a painful
one arrived; I kicked walls, guzzled
Feminax, keeled over in the bathroom.

I celebrated menopause by going floridly
mad; I'd no idea why my nightmares –
being set on fire, held under water – melded
with the experience of being awake. Everyone
was out to get us, to torture me and my son –
losing sight of myself still shapes me.

Karen Little

Dancing The Blood

Let's start with the women
who dance the red on the rocks
rich in iron in Pilbara.

They jump and stamp in a corroboree
of bouncing breasts as the blood
flows from them in streams
and ponds, lakes and rivers.

They are birthing the land,
right there at our beginnings.

Skip millennia to the no shame
women who dance the red
on the marathon streets of the city;

their iron steps proof that
if we run like Kiran Ghandi, our
wombs will not, in fact, fall out.

Blood overflows their shorts
blazing a wonderful trail.

Even Tracey's used tampons,
artful behind glass, the red
beginning to brown, are

dance step notations for blood.
Look. These are the old/new normal.

Kate Noakes

Doctor's Appointment

When did you stop? She asked
and I tried to remember when
that monthly offering to whatever
female god of fertility
had been withheld
and the lunar clock that is my body
failed to chime the twenty eighth
day of every month.

I know my lungs shrank with fear
that language would shrivel
with the womb – make me a
eunuch of poetry, an
incomplete woman, a writer
without the blood to write in.

But . . . the hand still reached for the pen,
and the brain, no longer confused by hormones,
cleared and steadied
knew the myth for what it was
and I had passed through smoke and fire
so lightly I could not remember
the hot coals under my feet –
only the purification and the gift.

Kathleen Jones

Paula Dunn

Menopause

The universe is an ovum
if we travel long enough we'll circle 'round & meet ourselves
holding a sign, 'Sex by Invitation only'

We burn our bras
bleed out our dreams using our baby-making bodies

      hi jinx & fashion is tomorrow's Bingo   comfortable shoes
                  stretchy waistbands and getting rid of hairs
                        under our nose & chinny chin chins
How do we begin in this unmapped country
hovering between gravestones and semi-detached estrogen
             where the bathroom mirror reflects an over-painted
                        unfinished

painting
                    of a woman we don't

know?

We wanted to be the girl from Ipanema
           so we made ourselves fuckable
But now her cool samba sweeps through us
sashaying with an invisible cloak
         of everyday & no one says
                'Ahh' anymore
as we float out to sea full of hotflash & spume
still wondering whether
        to spit or swallow.

Kathleen Strafford

Swung

In the red corridor of the shagging hotel
I stand, too bulging in the pink satin negligee
I chose because I thought the fleecy dressing gown
would make me look as mumsy and middle-aged
as I might feel.

I'm premenstrually bloated and pained
and paranoid I'll bleed early
in the nude pants wardrobe made me wear
which are ironically creating
lines that imply their existence.

I picture the shame of a spreading red stain,
standing among the women fit enough to wear
the black pvc and heels, tall enough to make
barefoot me a stumpy other, out of place
and unable to talk, too shy
to feel part of their fun-time frisson.

When I'd seen the writer's Facebook post
asking his edgy artsy friends to volunteer for this
it sounded so cool, a part of film history:

writers and artists and other cool acquaintances,
the reputed and the lesser known,
brought together like a 'Poets' Pub',

but extras in scenes of Scottish sexual politics,
Glasgow as 21st century backdrop:

nights and bodies and fun sex
and awkwardness,
love and impotence and hurt.

In the film I'll be only
a momentary pink satin blur
and my name won't be in the credits.

Katy Ewing

Pause For Thought

It was all I ever really wanted,
the flowering.
Blooming bright
red rose of life.
Not tiny buds, pricks, stick-thin
in a vest, second to last;
laughed at, shunned
unWoman.

Deadheaded, spent
at 52,
I still do.

Laura Taylor

Grand Climacteric

De-tuned from the sharp, metallic ring
of menarche to this molten pop and bubble,
the sly click of bones,
ears in the wrong key,
eyesight's descending scales.

My tongue sprouts bent wings,
clatters like dropped knives
or puddles to earth like a broken kite.
Words are snapped strings,
fingernails scraped down a blackboard.

I bring you seagulls tied up in bin bags,
rain on the roof, the smash of glass,
the slippery hollows of hot sighs
and sting of salt-smacked lips,
a whole orchestra of horny dissonance.

My finale almost brings the house down.

Lesley Quayle

The Okay Pokey – A Maenad Pausal Chant

You put your hormones in.
You pee your hormones out.
In, out, in, out – what's it all about?
You do the HRTy dirty
And you turn around.
That's what it's all about.
  Oh, oh, the HRTy dirty
  Whoah, the HRTy dirty
  Oh, oh, the HRTy dirty
  Knees ache, hips break,
  Bah, bah, bah.

You put your *fawnskin* on.
You wear your *fawnskin* out.
In, out, in, out, spread it all about.
You do the HRTy dirty
And you run around.
That's what it's all about.
  Oh, oh, the HRTy dirty
  Whoah, the HRTy dirty
  Oh, oh, the HRTy dirty
  Sweetcake, beefsteak,
  Rah, rah, rah.

You put your *thyrsus* in.
You take your *thyrsus* out.
In, out, in, out, can't get up the spout.
You do the HRTy dirty
And you don't slow down.
That's what it's all about.
  Oh, oh, the HRTy dirty
  Whoah, the HRTy dirty
  Oh, oh, the HRTy dirty
  Knees quake, hips shake,
  Aah, aah, aah.

Linda Goulden

The Lifesaving Discomfort

With the force of an anxious friend,
the cuff grips my arm.
Digits flash across the blank face.
I must keep pace – breathe myself
into a soothing rhythm.
The grip loosens, but my furious heart
betrays me, in my struggle to stay calm.
Systolic and diastolic pressures raised;
evidence that anxiety is battering against
my chest wall – beating my brain.
Her kind smile and reassurance see through
my false composure.
Since the laboratory results and appointment letter
were deposited on my doormat, *I have dreaded this.*
I'm usually sat in her place; hoping to appear reassuring,
teaching tools for living, forming change that is enduring.
Promoting self-care and self nurturing – to counteract anxiety
and keep hope growing; I know this – inside out.
I'm two years late for it, and feel rotten to the core.
I sniff, indignant, at this twisted irony; I don't always
practice what I preach, but it's cervical cancer prevention week.
Naked, from the waist to my feet, dignity preserved with a gown –
they guide me, gently, down,
legs spread wide, as the speculum forces openness;
to find the facts inside.
One in four women miss this, yet
anticipation was worse than reality.
A biopsy brings blood and an aching where I am hollow –
a hidden wound – where hope could grow.
I feel guilt, anger, fear –
then I remember,
I'm here
to fight it.
I smear my lipstick
and look to tomorrow.

Lorna Faye Dunsire

Late Developer

I was a *late developer*– I still hate that phrase –
It brings back to me my fifteen year old self,
with my child's body and a woman's brain.
Waiting, like a wrapped up Christmas present
for a garden of delights to emerge.

To be taken seriously, treated like an adult,
not overlooked and dismissed
like the teenager-child I appeared.
Some days I still think I'm waiting,
when testosterone driven bullish brutes
trample my opinions like snowflakes
or candy floss in hot water.

But I got there, more or less,
though the glance of some
tell me they think I'm still waiting –
I did get there.

The red cycle, motherhood,
breastfeeding my gifts –
two beautiful girls, now women themselves,
with women's bodies and wonderful opinions
and I cheer them on and watch in awe
as they carry the baton to the future.

Louise Dunsire

Menses

Moved by the moon
I feel the tide turn
Inside, the churn and gripe
The ache each month of an unmatched egg
Reluctant letting-go of another chance
The red badge of courage
For so many new beginnings

Lucy Jeynes

Blazing Trail

Twirled my torso from toilet bowl to wall of tiles and out it shot, a meaty spray like a slap of paint. Didn't mean to brandish my gold around like that, the functioning of my discrete insides. An uninterrupted line of slop, from bowl to drain to bathroom sides; it clung to the hairs down there, hairs already clinging to the drain's puckered eyes. And pride was what I felt, I feel, every time the gloop troops out of me. That thickness that passes, reminds: unrestrained, uncommodified. And I'm playing my lute like a mighty old organ, drip-filter flirting with the maybes of time. How many more years of this love-lust informance? How many cups could I fill if I stored them? Captured once, twice already – once by a box fish, but that's a whole other story, and once by my corking great child.

Lydia Unsworth

Text Book

It's just the perimenopause.
He said.
It's quite normal.
He said.
It can last up to a decade or so.
He said.
The good news is that you are not menopausal.
He said.

At that moment
I wished him Woman.

Lytisha Tunbridge

A Meal For One

Let's call the bowl a peace offering: *I bring you
this sorry weight.* A shiny steel resting place,
almost flawless in design-smooth edges, a sterile
surface where a cracked egg settles, perfectly
formed as it sways on a trolley, whipped out,
lapping at the cold touch, floppy, like raspberry jelly

infused with pomegranate; the last supper.
Wheels spin through corridors, flicking
back and forward, turning on themselves,
never changing direction. A man
in blue, hairnet clogs, checking his watch,
clock-off time, his retreat to normal life

catapulting this new time beyond
the bedside locker onto your bruised lap.
Think of a woman in stirrups, belly flat,
hope heavy, insides abandoned,
the hunger of the unbloody.

My Mother said if you have eggs
in the fridge, you have a meal.
She had five children.

Maeve McKenna

Conversations With My Father

Dad knew where to start
the bloody conversation
with Heinemann's 'What's Happening to Me?'
as our guide. We had chats
during my growing-up years.

He was clear:
this starting to bleed
once a month
was not an illness
just a change.

He bust old wife's tales,
didn't cringe, was his kindest,
and thought it absurd
women asked for pads
wrapped in brown paper bags
at Betty Kinnear's.

Maggie Mackay

The End Of Her Period Period

Picasso had his Blue period
mine was red, years and years of it
menstrual inspiration came only
every now and then, with no warning
once it lasted six weeks
mortification guaranteed
and pain, naturally (all too naturally)
only contraception helped

two sons later, back from a year's travel
in the 'third world' (don't ask)
hurtled into hospital
bleeding   :   unstoppable
Saturday night
wrong place   :   wrong time
they don't do ops on Sundays
(why? would God object?)

I begin to run out of blood
visiting friends notice
I seem to be going away
alarm   :   panic   :   transfusion
I vomit (must be alive, then)
hospital management relents, even though
it's not quite Monday yet

hysterectomy
the whole apparatus gone
no more bleeding, ever
anxious friends
how do you feel?
bloody amazing, I say
bloody amazing

Mandy Macdonald

First Blood

After The Stain On The Cotton Sheet
the mother stands with her child

finger on lips by the linen cupboard
while the father, curled like a dog

night-shift-sleeps under the counterpane
his photo on the mantelpiece

above the fire the mother has built
of twisted paper under clods of coal.

The child wrapped in a spinning
top of dreams

peeks in the book secreted on the shelf
among Holy Bibles and commentaries.

Outside in the garden
among winter's thorns
berries shine like rubies.

Marg Roberts

Our Courses

Begin with no celebration.
A silent secret cut-mark, red.
Hormone flow, an introduction
to womanhood, bringing a pang
of unexpected shock and shame.
Despite mothers' preparation.
No warning can inform reaction
to menstrual cycle, the 'normal
pattern of flow', as though we could
knit it into a thing to wear.
Instead we tighten hideous belts,
carry pads like rough bricks of shame.
Shrink inside, hide exposure fear,
arch backs and limbs when tough pain comes
with dreaded dysmenorrhea.
Crying, we curl with hot bottles.
Drained, we pop pills, wilt in the heat,
feel the pendulous weight of pain
ricochet our sombre mood-swings
then we grow psycho-killer wings.

The final debacle of menstrual cycle
is constant surprise of irregularity.
Courses change without dignity or decency.
Do not pack a bag and leave, but sail on unplanned
tides of blood red rivers; floods that could not be staunched,
changes come like the monsoon rain after the heat
and without warning, so, lack of preparation
leaves us diminished, feeling finished as women.
Discarded unwanted. Left with our anxieties
of the lost course.
I don't miss it.
I wish it goodbye.

Margaret Rowland

When A Butch Finds Her Blousy Side In Her Menopausal Lover.

Up to now, not to know when it was coming was a secret badge of honour:
No dread, no fear of mood swings,
Sometimes a punch to the stomach felt,
Discreetly giving in to writhing in a darkened room,
But a virile swim, a bike ride put paid to any suffering.
No PMT was clocked, I wouldn't care if I was in your face just before,
I wouldn't notice. Oblivious fuss free menstruating was my thing.
Now with a sexy, menopausal woman for a wife, life's made me louche and
blousy,
Consciously blood lairy, my monthly sanguinity's a red and rosy choir,
Bursting blood cells a celebration in her arms, they blast
Mammoth harmonies to resonate inside our cavern mouths,
And I relish the surge coursing through my pelvis like a spring's rush,
More volume to pulsate our rocking, power to my stallion loins in lust,
Rip roar to my butch and bloody victory charge,
Revolution crowds to storm sex palaces in winter.
My girl's delicious, cheeky, I may still bleed but she's so over that,
Hormones don't take her like a crass highwayman, the tolls I've still to pay.
Secretly, I harbour fantasies I bleed for two, juicing her with my cherry lips.
Menopausal she may be, but our lubrication factory
Jaw drops me with fruitiness in valleys, folds and forms.
Hot flushes crown us her seeds of crone energy,
I clothe her in my fecund robes and generous realms,
King her on rich volcanic plains. She queens me with imagined heirs.
So our chapters of womanhood merge in blood shared
Making us a raging bull of female power, begotten, blooming
Blood sisters and full blown wombs for each other,
Eternal twins hugging in our cushioned canal of becoming,
Our wall to wall mothering, plush, plump, naive and winning,
Blushing in each other's joy in living, like two flush
Ruddy cheeks on a Siberian morning.

Maria Andrews

Rats

She's trying the door again, rattling the handle.
She's wearing her old blue slippers. Not the new ones
her brother bought her. The rip and suck of worn out
soles shuffle back and forth across the cold lino.
Hunched shoulders, arms crossed tight, pain rising.
Head down she knows every inch of this sticky floor.
Angular shoulders, hollow bones light as air, want to stretch.
Nylon stockings slip to bunches at her ankles. The starched,
standard issue, two sizes too big floral dress, billows and tugs.

He's watching, feet up on the desk. The clip, clip
of nicotine stained nails ricocheting across the desk.
Chair tipped back. He can watch her, door open.
Bunch of keys dangling from under his paunch.
The grey crumple of his Charge Nurse's uniform
trousers bulging, pockets stuffed with boiled sweets, fags.
He hates nights, hates mixed wards, hates women and
it's a full moon. Nymphos all of them. She'll be as high
as a kite soon. Go see what she wants.

I know what she wants. The locked door marked STORE.
It won't be open til Monday. Tomorrow's Sunday. Tomorrow
her brother comes to take her out. They walk in the grounds
past groaning bushes. A naked foot, an unlaced shoe. A trail
of stocking caught like a brown tail in the undergrowth.
I open the door, hand her a packet of Dr.Whites. She'll stuff
as many as she can in her knickers. I once handed her tampons
but she screamed. Read her notes. Admitted age 19yrs,
23years ago. Agitated. Says she has rats in her vagina.
Repeatedly self-harms in genital area. Paranoid delusions.

Marion Oxley

Confession

Here is my confession
To an odd club I belong:
I regularly realise that
My tampon's in wrong.

Perhaps it's my method,
My dexterity the flaw,
But it's a pet peeve of mine
In this monthly menses bore.

There are other more pressing
Important symptoms to bear
Still I'd welcome a support group
For rummaging *down there*.

I'm not saying YouTube
Photo guides, or *How To*
Just some gentle encouragement
When I'm off to the loo.

We are forced to hide our periods
Out of mind and out of sight
But in this safe space, let me tell you:
My tampon's not in right.

Martha Flower

Kunda

The soul of the world lies in my womb cave   carnelian curd rises with tides
to flow into psychic ripples   that begin with shimmering wisdom
        emerging from the primordial sea

i float in enlightened power   journeying through the cosmos
        past the yonic wounds of the universe   into the healing of sa

thus landed on the island of my vulva i
gather the blossom of my Cunti
        anoint my third eye with my moonblood

travel seeing earth as earth, water as
        water my bleeding as humanity's pain and suffering
                flowing out into healing   rivers of transformation

Maya Chowdhry

Big Meaty Things

Truth came, like an angel –
with wings. Until then, I'd thought it was just me:
I was as twisted as my pad usually ended up,

a soggy lump that couldn't staunch anything, collapsed
in on itself, or tits up with the gum strip stuck to my pubes
(though I never used those words then,
kept my mouth as clean as I wanted my pants to be).

Just me whose thighs wouldn't behave
(big meaty things, they moved when I walked -
how was my pad supposed to stay still with my defective moving thighs?),
just me who had to poke my fingers in my knickers
when no-one was looking, tug at the edges to make sure,
or wiggle about on my seat to try to flatten it out,
just me who had a monstrous drooling mouth
that lipstick-snogged my gusset.

But then wings appeared
on the market, with an annunciation:
no-one could get the bloody things to work.
It was a universal problem, a design fault,
to which they now offered a solution.
Womanhood itself had to be glued down,
tucked under at the edges, or it would start
wandering off.

Melanie Branton

Eve's Punishment

On all fours like a dog,
I'm crawling, crying.
I can't speak.

You find me there,
trembling,
do you shout?

Do you beg?
How is anybody
supposed to know,

this is just what
a woman deserves
inside her skin.

A pomegranate
of hellfire
all her own.

Miranda Lynn Barnes

The Curse

Signs of a new life
disappearing
bright cascades
splashing
on barren rocks below.

Each ferrous lunar lake left behind
I had to tread, re-tread the path,
without waymarks.

My womb howled.
I tried out spells
from a wise woman who offered remedies

aborted on the tongue,
from a magician boasting a screen,
searching for an open route.

The fig tree saved us on this odyssey
as Poseidon, you navigated
the sea-storm, sailed inland,
landing sinuous, on to the shore.

Moira Garland

Your Period Came To Woolacombe

You were twelve. For the first time, you noticed
the grimy shallowness of the outdoor pool,
its tired tiles, its cigarette ends,
its blurred escaped receipts.

At the beach, you pictured boats being wrecked
on Hartland Point's serrated knife.
The lighthouse's star shook.
Mist smuggled Lundy over the horizon.

Here, you'd only bled once before –
you'd cut your foot on a snaggletooth of shell,
and the sea foam, which you'd known was the dissolved bones
of dead mermaids, had gushed forward
to make it sting. You'd yowled then,

but now, you were twelve. You wanted to plunge
through water with jellyfish toddlers, yet
you pushed this urge back up, against its threat to spill.

Shrivelled under the rain, tight as barnacles,
your grandparents ate sandwiches and scones.
You lay like a beached haddock, eyes glazed;
mouth gaping, downturned.
The tide came in whenever you moved.

Olivia Tuck

All The Things

no-one told you that you would need
to remember the date of your last period
how in your twenties and thirties
there would be times when
bleeding was good (not pregnant)
and when it wasn't (the blue stripe)
life (blood) gushed her exuberance
through your forties in front
of a class or at a conference
in your fifties life (blood)
drowned the fattest tampon
she gifted ruby clots pulled your guts
apart and stained every chair
your black trousers stank
your back ached and flooded
with (blood) lust you wanted
to fuck men who loved doing it
when you were on and those who didn't
you wanted to drench every bed
to turn the floors of their houses into crime scenes

#

she kept you guessing
it's over you thought
then life (blood) sputtered on
through night sweats
and horny dreams
then one day
a simple test said
all your oestrogen had gone

sad and relieved
you are not done with life

Pam Thompson

Misconception

There was un-used storage capacity
she never stretched into function.
All the times its lining came away,
washed her bloody insides out.

Voices chatter like the unborn
in the canteen of her womb,
speculate about management
decisions made in the bedroom.

If there had been mechanical
failure, surely engineers would
have worked all night to fix
her fault, restore productivity.

Was she not in a militant union
with a shop steward prepared
to fight, call time on inaction.
Solidarity is a fluttering standard.

Wasn't it in her job description,
paragraph 24, clause 16, after
the bit about clocking off before
the caretaker leaves at midnight.

People were nice to her when
she was issued with redundancy
but they gave her a life-like doll
that sang *ma-ma* when dropped.

Pat Edwards

Those Bloody Visitors Again

Like all the best unwanted guests
they turned up too early. Before the childhood chores
were finished; your body's cushions not yet plumped.
You were told "That's how it is. They come
whether you like it or not. Be ready."

Their early visits so unpredictable. Arriving
at the most inconvenient times – making worse
days of exams or stage shows or excruciating first dates.
Until they settled into a routine; regularity with a price
of bad behaviour: trashing the house, cramping you with sly violence.

You heard of women who sounded lucky,
some circumstance of birth or surgery leaving them unvisited.
But like a patient lying alone in a hospital bed
you knew they would rather have had a crush
of noisy interruptions than such unchosen and solitary rest.

As with any frequent guest, familiarity bred
contempt and for a while you found a blister-packed way
of taming their worst excesses, pinning them
to their scheduled dates, holding their punches at arm's length.
Too soon you are too old.

So it is back to guesswork and hope. Okay at first,
like a family reunion before the accusations start.
Then a lifetime of bodily recriminations flooding out
worse than ever and still so bloody inconvenient.
Always on wedding days and holidays and Ofsted weeks and –

That's enough.
You hear of an escape from this biological obligation.
A permanent eviction effected by Our Lady of Mirena.
After which you are easily able to slam the door
in their nauseating faces and leave the whole pack of bastards
standing gobsmacked on the step.

Penny Blackburn

Tree Song

In the Moluccas girls gather
when their blood flows

girls gather when warm winds
blow their sarongs

yellow blossom sings
Molucca   Molucca

Molucca brings girls to gather
when their blood sings

when clove-trees blossom
their scent calls girls to sing

as blood flows girls sing
wind blows under sarongs

and yellow blossom calls
to them in the Moluccas

Penny Sharman

First published in The Writer's Café Magazine:

Exhibition

Her still life deposits
left on knicker seats,
in porcelain bowls,
are unseen spectrums of colour.
But he won't see her art
tarnish those luxury Grecian
sheets. He tri-folds

a towel that shrieks
of branded mule, brags how
she's quite the little savage
for wanting it all month long, then
shields his eyes when he pulls out.
He can't look at what she
is, who might have been:

a baby's florid pink chamber
rinsing from the womb.
He'll tell her he likes how she talks
from between her thighs, vulgar.
She bleeds out stories with
upon a time stains:
boysenberries, black jam,

little lost reds,
dusky oaks of Syrah.

Rachael Smart

First Period

My grandfather tells me to go home
I swallow the lump in my throat,

I'm looking forward to watching
John Wayne in *True Grit* on the telly.

My grandfather can't look me in the eye
and says it's for the best.

My grandmother gives me a pad
with a loop and a belt,

prays five Hail Mary's for me
and says the Lady Immaculate

on the stairway is crying tears of joy
and pain because periods

are both a blessing and a curse.

Rachel Burns

Moon Landing: The Last

I'm preparing for lift off from Kos, haven't moonwalked in months, surprised to get the call-up. The *Bodyform* machine at launch pad isn't working. I'm hoping Mission Control will be prepared but *we don't keep them on board – most Kosmonauts bring their own.* I tell her my body's a tsunami, so she says she'll decommission the cubicle at the rear of the shuttle. She brings me paper towels. My lack of *sang froid* affronts her: she's all but a moon novice, doesn't know yet how moonwalking is a bloody messy job. I want to tell her – if she hasn't learned from her own moon training – that when a menopausal Kosmonaut talks of floods it's not hyperbole. I try to stand up but the gloopy gush of blood between thighs is gravity, keeping me in my seat. Trolley Dolly tells me to hurry, she can't keep the washroom free all flight. In the next seat, my friend puts a hand up her own skirt, pulls down her knickers hands them to me. I trap a wad of tissues in her pants as I pull them up over my own. Knees together, I moonwalk the shuttle's length to the ladies, where my body disgorges pigs' liver the size of a baby's head. On my return to Earth, the medical officer stands me down from all future moon landings.

Rachel Davies

Paula Dunn

Donegal 1992

The girl's on fire duty; kindles up sparks and baby flares.
We fetch her twigs and turf from barrows we wheeled
from bog to shore, glad they've had a year to dry.

We weave Pound Shop blankets, diamond patterned,
through poles we borrowed from harbours down the coast.
Fettle windbreaks despite the rising easterly.

A rag of song escapes from someone's keeping, and though
it's not time to sing yet, tunes ribbon through us.
Half the notes are from now, half from time's start,

innate, re-found. Someone reckons she sees sea lions
on the horizon, the rest that she's an optimist
on eggnog. We tally the heavens, bright, unashamed,

not a cloud to spare their blushes. Just what we ordered
when we were playing at omnipotence for this, this
crimson dark. Behind us the Atlantic stills as it turns.

Signal to let loose the anthem no-one composed,
but known to us all. Our girl,–she's allowed
as many mothers as she needs tonight –

looks for our nod, unwraps a tight twist of good tweed,
lets fall a cotton plug stained claret. It shimmies in the heat,
catches. Its smoke, neither acrid nor sweet, doesn't last.

Dancing was planned on the flame-warmed rock.
Instead, we sync breath, link fingers, make wishes
on long dry bones and our mothers' anxious shame.

Rebecca Bilkau

Operating Lair

As if a small wolf has crept inside,
breathing under the three-armed
hospital gown I scent danger
creeping through my skin. I'm trussed up
in white compression socks as though my legs
are flags of surrender. A nurse holds my arm
as she leads me up the stairs in case I think twice.

I ask the anaesthetist if he is sure
I will come round
as he inserts a cannula into a blood vessel
through the tough skin on the back of my hand.
The oxygen mask traps my face.
His answer: Are you afraid?
makes me think of my wombwolf.
I don't mention her,
hoping they won't hurt her
when they open me up,
or drag her out of my innerds
and replace her with stones.

I answer But I'm not yet gone.
He says You will be soon …
it's coming now.

Rebecca Gethin

Double Period Maths

I'm huddling at the too-small desk,
shivering beside the radiator,
trying not to cry as I sense the blood
trickling down my thighs.

Mr Birch bores on about Euclidean solids
while I wonder how to bear this dragging pain.
Count up and down the waves, breathe,
fumble in my satchel for clean sanitary towels,
fold one, left-handed, slip it into my skirt pocket.

I give brief attention to an isoceles triangle,
between roaring tides of pain. This is
the stark red reality under the pink lace lie.
Please sir, I gasp, giving in, can I leave the room?

I hobble out, hoping no blood stains
on the back of my skirt give the boys
an excuse to snigger their hateful
'jamrag, jamrag, she's riding the rag' ...
out through the rain to the filthy lavs,
away from the cool elegance of theorems.

I wrap the evidence in school issue Jeyes,
clean myself up as best I can, watch
the blood flow and clot into the toilet,
black, brown, dark red. It's so cold in here.
Leaning my head against the cubicle door,
I will myself not to faint on the filthy floor.

By the time I get back to Euclid, blood
will be seeping around the sanitary towel
again. But no more head-banging,
just gritting the teeth, acting like
nothing's going on, back to proving
the theorem: girls are no good at geometry.

Rosemary McLeish

Eggs At Rinrow

Was it winter? It was dark before we'd
left the sands, the days ending cut with
salt-sharp longing at my cousin Sally's offer,
to skinny dippy with her boyfriend.
Her lure to the waves floated high
above us that night, high as silk bubbles
kissing the waters of the Atlantic.
I felt queasy, spinning above those
waves in my mind, unsure of my
chances of floating. Was I bleeding?
Mortified by explaining the pad, the blood,
the hair, I didn't even say no. Didn't even
mention the Sharks some other cousin had
spotted that summer. We quite believed them.
I wasn't quite sixteen, and still
at the stage of hiding the covers of
illicit Mills-and-Boon paperbacks
away from my mothers gaze, in
infallible brown envelopes.

My cousin Sally had all the tricks to
show me. So Sally had poured in vodka with
my orange juice. Which was fine
until my mum got thirsty, drank,
declared the fruit sour.
Was it a summers day off Rinroe, or
did the sun bounce off the sand dunes
and into my eyes the day we found the
eggs already cold on the beach.
Hole half-dug, sand scattered everywhere.
My uncle was all for putting them into the
hotpress to see what came out.
But my cousin Tommy, desperate
for warm socks, put his hands through
them, quite by accident.
I stayed by the range that night,
the night Sally flew naked
into the Atlantic.

S M Jenkin

1954 – A Period Of Time

My first day at the new comprehensive
and I don't want to take a communal shower.
I'm eleven and small for my age.
Miss says showers are compulsory after Games
unless I produce a note from a parent
to state, it is my period of time.

Mam's no help. She stubs her woodbine
in the ashtray and tells me she'll buy
a packet of Kotex and a belt. She believes
in Baden-Powell's motto and when I finally start,
I'll need to stop playing with lads –
even Derek.

There's blood on my knickers and I think
I'm on my way to Heaven. I tell Derek.
He says he'll miss me, but would I mind asking Angie
to help him with his maths when I'm gone.
Next day he tells me his mother thinks it unwise
to invite me to tea

which is what she said when I caught nits.
I'm scared. My belly aches.
Mam says it's normal, but I mustn't wash my hair
or take a bath. I cry. I suspect I'll be too dirty
to be allowed through the pearly gates.

Derek's sister came to my rescue.
She sneaked a book into my satchel.
It explained how girls are transformed into women.
Inside the front cover there was a handwritten note –
After reading please pass to a friend.

Sandra Burnett

One For Mad Lights

After coming off the pill you are back.

I know when you are coming.
You are less predictable than monthly now.

My vision is taken one pixel at a time.
I avoid bright lights
and low winter sun.
I wear sunglasses in fluorescent-high offices.
Because these are to you like an invitation to a vampire.

Until you flood my vision with darkness.
Until you drain the pink from my skin.
Until you lead me to a curtained room
as this is the only place I can exist
until you are gone.

Sarah L Dixon

Cursed

I rummage in my bag,
pretend to look for something,
a pen,
a piece of paper –
anything.

I slip a tampon up my sleeve,
make some excuse about
needing to see someone
and half-run down the corridor,
hoping there's nobody behind me

to see the stain of womanhood:
a bleeding scab on the back
of your teacher's skirt.

Sarah Miles

Chhaupadi

He knew it was illegal and did not say anything,
even though the winter was so bitter.
But the collective memory was strong
and his silence told her what she needed to know.
The blot on her skirt
was a stain on her soul
so she left the house until she was 'clean'.
The tiny shed was so so cold
she lit a fire and closed the door against the snow and wind,
breathing in toxic warmth until it stayed her chest.
Afterwards the villagers destroyed all the sheds
but the lingering habit will take years to fade.
And in the meantime,
every month,
her husband is haunted
by the smothering aroma of the smoke that killed her.

Sarah Wragg

Lessons Learned

From the age of eleven to sixteen, she spent a day
    each month rolling or foetal in the school sickbay
discovering that dysmenorrhea wasn't an illness,
    that vomiting and sweats weren't reasons to fuss.
This was what it meant to be a woman, so she must
    get used to it, get on with it, keep quiet – just
catch up on missed periods, not play the martyr.

    She must cope with bulk, belt, leak; master
the skill of laundering knickers to banish stains,
    cherish whiteness; must not flirt with tampons,
never arouse herself with unseemly self-contact,
    nor risk breaking what needed to remain intact –
silence, maidenhead, whatever. And she should
    never bring trouble home, ruin her childhood.

Sharon Larkin

Birthday Roses

After I'd freed them
from their cellophane bandage
they blazed with the colour
hidden under my skirt.

I swallowed two Feminax
and fetched paper and pen.
*My love, my darling, thank you
for the beautiful bouquet.*

He couldn't have known
I'd circled the nineteenth
of July in my diary
and scrawled *period due.*

He couldn't have guessed
I'd hunch on the sofa, nurse
gut-gripes and backache
as I gazed at twelve red roses

that claimed the windowsill,
their petals tightly-whorled
and plusher than velvet,
their stems water-shone

as though in celebration
of the pull of the tide
and my body's obedient gush:
its final blood-fall

until our daughter was lifted
into May's morning light
and wore crimson ribbons
untied from my womb.

Sheila Jacob

Rhinoceros

Rhinoceros pre/occupies you, bulges you
with clamped clog-body, heavy-treading,

this slowly-swingeing, odd-toed ungulate,
weak-eyed, small-brained, rage-charged,

undigested matter sludged in its hindgut,
scarry skin too cracked for stroking

you wait   you wait   you wait

for nothing to happen

Shelley Tracey

New Territory

In the waiting room, I thumb
through magazines, prepare
for results, wonder if I should check
my blood pressure on the free machine.

You are post-menopausal
is a thunderclap repeated.
I hear it,
but it doesn't sink in.

My womb is empty. A cavern
where blood no longer flows.
Each egg expired, a raging
furnace rising from toes to hair.

Walking home, a storm is brewing.
Each tree, each leaf, made new
by a change in the air.

Sheryl McMahon

Blasphemy

In the beginning, before she had begun
to bleed, before she had learnt to speak
her Mother-tongue, they silenced her.
Cut out her tongue. Named her
in the language of their Gods:
the shame of Eve, the fall of man, the devil's gateway.
For forty years – and centuries more – she spoke
no word. Caught
in the muttered incantation of a diabolic curse.
It took a while to learn a different verse,
it took a while to grow another tongue –
at first it stuck and stuttered in her jaw,
it clogged and cluttered in her craw,
spat out words like bitch and slag and whore.

For forty years - and centuries more – she bled
each month and heard a word, a phrase, a fragment
of a rhyme – a half-remembered sentence
of her own. For forty years – and centuries more –
she learnt her language well; this blood-line lexicon
of hers that lives within her flesh, and now she knows
the thousand names of God; they breathe beneath her skin
each one a song, a rose, a burning hymn.
Now, when she speaks, rivers flow
from her open mouth, mountains blaze
with fire, the Gods themselves lie down
upon her feet and know her name
to be Desire. For in the beginning, was the word
made flesh between her open legs; the Logos
of all life and birth and death.

Her body is a holy book.
Her language is a-flame.

Siobhan Mac Mahon

The First Flush

She went with the startling murmuration
of the first flush, left you low and dry,
clutching at the brittle bones of beauty.
You caught a glimpse of her heels
rounding the corner of your mind,
grasped at her skirt as she slipped,
fleeting as days, into the lie of shadows.

You played a daily game
of hide and seek; tried to coax her out
from the hollow of your cheek,
sweep her back in with a blusher brush.

You huff the glass to a frosty moon,
trying to read the lines she wrote you.
Epiphany shuffles in, slipper-shod,
stuffs the shapeless pulp of your heart
into a stranger's body – knits a baggy blouse
from the ravel of your brow,
casts you off with the yarn of youth.

Stella Wulf

Patience

That morning, after twenty thousand days
of wounds and oversights,
preconceptions, prejudices, slights,
leers that morphed to jeers,
echoing her buttocks down the street,
of fingers that presumed entitlement,
days of tenderness, of raw emotion,
days of speculum and speculation,
wombfuls of sea-urchins, gnawing aches;
somewhere between gravid and the grave,
patience turned to pyroclastic flow.

Forensic studies of her transformation
searched the smouldering slopes for evidence,
for the catalyst, the rift, the source that sparked
the lava flooding, raging, from her core.
She herself could comprehend no more than science,
only felt the sudden heat,
the swollen, shifting nature of her shape,
the molten language rising,
the raw, unscheduled candour of the roar,
blistering the tongue so long contained.
Patience erupted. A mountain remained.

Su Ryder

The Curse

She is all woman now,
daughter become sister,
spindle-prick of peony
smearing her whites.

A butterfly wing of bright
crimson surprises her waking,
shyly she comes to me bringing
her ring-o'roses, her scarlet bouquet.

We are joined in blood
by the slow pull of the moon's
waning, the small secrets
of darkened bathroom shelves.

How the past echoes. My mother's
silent mouthing of those witchcraft
words, The Curse, as she taught me
to name that first staining.

Have we forgotten those
cackle voices; conspiratorial whispers
echoing among unguents and tinctures
in white-tiled rooms?

And I who was mute, spineless
as a seahorse, wish you brave
and beautiful. Feel your roots, deep
and damp as rusty beets smelling of earth.

Sue Hubbard

Women's Troubles

Whispers. Hushed telephone calls,
Time-of-life, the-change. Women's troubles.
Me sent with notes to the chemist's –
twelve Lilia towels, Extra Large.
Handed over the counter in a brown paper bag.

Be-a-good-girl ... pull-your-weight...be-nice-to-your-mother.
Me trying not to gag at the rank stink of soiled sanitary towels
stashed under her bed, embarrassed
by furtive late night bonfires in the back garden.

Then
the word they wouldn't say.
No, they haven't told her...it's best that way.
Cancer.
Susan doesn't know.

[With the visceral ache of adolescent resentment]
Me, left to buy my own Lilia towels, with loops.
To work out the knack of hanging them on an
elastic suspender belt, carry their bulk in thick navy knickers.
Repelled by the acrid stench of school incinerators.

Me, left to grow up with a deep dread of menopause,
and overwhelming grief for what I never said,
what she was never allowed to say.

Sue Mackrell

I Want A Parrot

I've started wanting a parrot
I go to the local Bird House
and watch them climb with their beaks

Perhaps it's the luminous vibrancy
or the way they look at you, as if they
know how you like your eggs,
or how you touch your face when you are nervous

I touch my face because I am always nervous,
I have hives, is it the menopause
or am I just highly strung?

Now, a flutter of sparrows lift up from
as many nests as there are leaves on the ivy.
I'm sure I am with them
until I see my feet on the ground

I want a parrot,
its claws on my shoulder gripping me in this world,
me launch pad, me ground, me tree,
the solid me to its bird.

Maybe I just want someone to talk to.

Susannah Violette

Flawed Mechanics

Not wanting to pack anything that might
remind me, I left the blue plastic sponge bag
with its sour scent of Imperial Leather,

three unread magazines and the paperback
copy of *Catch 22*, stashed them in the broken locker
with unwanted grapes and bruised peaches.

Not wanting prescriptions of age related shame
the gynaecologists dispensed, I plugged in
ear buds, turned up the volume on *Gimme Shelter,*

transfused their womb of sterile language,
discarded that egg-shaped pebble I had so long tried
to swallow. Adopted a menopausal smile.

Tina Cole

Sonnet For Women Of A Certain Age

Fear not the menopause but celebrate
the ending of your fertile years.
Your shrivelled womb means happy days to come
of even-tempered mood, no monthly tears.
As well as saving cash on tampons, pads and such
you'll find that facial spots will go, your skin look smashing.
Your hair, once greasy, flat and dull
will bounce with health and need less frequent washing.
Your hair, perhaps, will grey and sprout upon your chin
but body smells will lessen now as pheromones decline.
You'll worry less, you'll find that life is fun
and everything around you feel a bit benign.
So don't regret the losses, celebrate the gains
and worry not – sexual desire remains!

Tonnie Richmond

First Spell

If we can magic our first bleed into being
then I am guilty of witchcraft. I conjured it
from articles in magazines, whispers
from cousins and sisters who bloomed
on each new moon, the colour of the inside
of the mouth, the shape of a river slipping
into estuaries, flowing into the world
sure and hot. Magicked from words
spoken by kind school nurses,
the diagrams I brought home
the afternoon we got the talk,
swinging my little parcel like candy,
the word in my stomach, rolling
off my lips like an incantation:
period, period, period.

Tracey Rhys

The Red Scarf

on menopause

I picked up
the knitting needles
skein of red yarn
began to knit a scarf
that grew and grew
with my skin and blood
threaded through
until one day
the red ran out
the scarf unraveled
the fibers scattered
the knitting needles
       I put down

Tricia Marcella Cimera

Letter To My Son

All my life, I waited
to love this body,
with its darkness and magic,
its bad blood.

I feared the life it bore, afraid
it would rip away your little being,
leave me empty, a skin-bag
on the ebbing tide.

It was easier to love with you
hidden within the cells of me
but you grew, insistent of leaving,
pushing against possibilities

until there you were, eyes black
as the night that bore them,
my cry still wet on your mouth,
a whole life ahead of you.

Just as you were once new born,
so am I returning to the birth of me,
becoming crone-bird, silver-seal,
slipping quietly into sea.

I remember now, something
of the she who walked barefoot,
strong legs dancing over bones.
I catch scent of her, remember

that *she* is me, that the darkness
is not stinking. It is life –
the stone, the blood, the bone,
all those things I made you from:

beautiful, mighty, strong.

Victoria Bennett

These Days

A morning quickie
Is off the menu
These days.

My body
Once so generous
With her vital juices
Has drawn them deep
Into her core
To use for other purposes
These days.

She will relent
And yield them up
If time, and due respect
Are given
(And perhaps a little
Supplementation
From other sources
If you get my meaning.)

So, when the fancy takes us
We have to set aside
A whole afternoon:
Like a vintage classic
My 0-60 is leisurely
Pleasurely
These days.

Victoria Riddiford

Menopause

Later, looking back
She could identify the moment.

Wellbeing suddenly swept away
By the bullying
Side-swipe of the headache.
An ordinary Friday afternoon,
Taking the children for routine optometry.
Nausea rising in bile, vision splintered
By shards of brilliant blindness.

Driving home via McDonalds
To excuse herself from cooking,
Longing limply for the undemanding comfort
Of the abandoned marital bed.

In the night suddenly wide awake,
Her skin a living forcefield,
Every pore charged with a tiny pin prick shock,
Each shock generating a diamond bead of sweat,
A million droplets coalescing into
Spontaneous total immersion.
Hell's baptism
On the coldest night of the year.

Wendy-Jane Walton

Red Dragon

I was 10 years old and in foster care when the red dragon first arrived,
staining sheets where I slept, causing panic and confusion.
My foster-mother's eyes narrowing in disgust as she stripped
                                        me of my dignity
as well as the bed, placing the soiled bedding into a bucket under the sink.
My nightdress, crimson like the embarrassed glow on my cheeks
like the angry redness of her face when she told me how much extra work
                                        I caused her.
Denying my stricken questions with a withering look.
A trip to Boots for Dr White's and a blue sanitary belt with hooks.
I walked like John Wayne with the bulkiness between my legs and I was
                                        the only one in my class
with a satchel full of 'jam rag' indicators.
I was only 3,650 days old and the men had just landed on the moon.
Every month the red dragon would bring cramping, clotting and bloating,
My foster-mother told me I was now a 'woman' but how could that be?
I still played with Tiny Tears and built walls with Lego but
                                        her mouth formed a thin line
of disapproval when she told me, so it must've been true.
I was the 'bothersome' child that she 'rescued' from the Children's Home,
now I had become an annoying, bleeding woman-child with stained
                                        underwear and tears.
I told no-one of the torment and anguish of the red dragon's
                                        unwelcome visits
or of how 'dirty' and 'disgusting' I was made to feel
by the woman who should've loved me enough to explain it all.
Thank God for the menopause when the red dragon left my life for good

Yvonne Ugarte

(ˈWʊmən)

A garbage dumped foetus wrapped
in the Hindustan Times or,
luckier, tweeting and
menarchial, learning
not to wear white skirts
to avoid trouble, knowing
the cramps of expectation;
adequate adult female,
bitch, queer, trans, cis, lezzy, quine,
Shakti in high heels, lipsticked,
blow-dried, stubbled, smoothed, pulsing
brain big as a universe,
abdomen like a planet
squeezing all life out of her,
queen of metamorphosis
swelling and contracting to
a chamber ripe with endings,
Ishtar, Freya, crone casting
poppies on a winding sheet
cackling at definition

Morag Smith

Short Biographies

Agnes Marton's recent publications include her collection *Captain Fly's Bucket List* and four chapbooks with Moria Books. She won the National Poetry Day Competition.

Alex Josephy lives, disrobes and writes in London and Italy. Her latest collection, *Naked Since Faversham*, was published by Pindrop Press in May 2020.

Ali Jones' work has been widely published in journals and online. She has two pamphlets, *Heartwood*, and *Omega*, with Indigo Dreams Press. Her first collection is forthcoming with Hedgehog Press.

Alwyn Marriage's 11 books include poetry, fiction and non-fiction. She is Managing Editor of Oversteps Books and research fellow at Surrey University. www.marriages.me.uk/alwyn

Angela Serena Gilmour lives by herself amongst the forests and lakes on the outskirts of Berlin. Biology be damned, she is finally becoming who she was supposed to be.

Angi Holden writes adult and children's poetry and fiction. She won the MMB Poetry Pamphlet Prize for *Spools of Thread* and the Victoria Baths Splash Fiction Prize.

Anna Cole is a teacher and poet from Bradford, West Yorkshire.

Anna Kisby is a Devon-based poet, archivist, mother of three, and author of the pamphlet *All the Naked Daughters* (Against the Grain Press, 2017).

Anne Caldwell is based in West Yorkshire. She has published two poetry collections with Cinnamon and will have a new book of prose poems in late 2020, *Alice and the North*. (Valley Press).

Anne McMaster lives on an old farm in Northern Ireland. Her debut collection *Walking Off the Land* will be published by Hedgehog Poetry Press in late 2020.

B. Anne Adriaens' work reflects her interest in the weird and dark. She's written several environmental dystopian pieces and is finalising her first poetry collection.

Barsa Ray is published in Magma, Filigree (Peepal Tree), Watch the Birdie; filmed for the Yorkshire Arts Festival; performed at East Leeds FM, Ilkley and Bradford Lit Fests.

Becky Cherriman is a community-minded writer, wild swimmer & Teaching Fellow @ UniversityofLeeds. Pamphlet – *Echolocation*. Collection – *Empires of Clay*. http://www.beckycherriman.com/

Bee Smith works at Word Alchemy in the bucolic splendour of an Irish geopark; blogs as sojourningsmith; creative writing coach in schools, prisons, art centres, online.

Bev Morris fidgets. Poetry, flash fiction, script, dystopian novels – she'll have a crack at anything. Currently writing the life story of a special forces operative.

Carole Bromley lives in York. 3 collections with Smith/Doorstop, a pamphlet, *Sodium 136*, with Calder Valley and a new book *September* with Valley Press. Hamish Canham winner.

Caroline Gilfillan has published four poetry collections. She's now working on poems about the Women's Liberation Movement of the 1970s. www.carolinegilfillan.co.uk

Caroline Hardaker lives in Newcastle and is a poet, novelist, librettist, and amateur puppeteer. Discover her books and adventures at www.carolinehardakerwrites.com.

Char March started writing poems at 5; bleeding at 12; wanted it all out at 22; stopped at 52; still hot-flushing (et al) at 59. Poem awards yes, but wants a bloody medal!

Charlotte Ansell lives on a boat on the Medway & is currently navigating the murky waters of perimenopause. Her 3rd collection *Deluge* was a 2019 PBS recommendation.

Chaucer Cameron is a poet, her latest work *Wild Whispers*, a poetry-film collaboration, was recommended for the Ted Hughes Award. Chaucer is co-editor of Poetry Film Live.

Cheryl Pearson lives in Manchester. She is the author of *Menagerie* (The Emma Press, 2020) and *Oysterlight* (Pindrop Press, 2017).

Chris Grogan lives in Yorkshire. When she's not writing or painting you can find her on the fells.

Christina Wilson is a mother and poet from Yorkshire. She facilitates therapeutic writing groups and is beginning a PhD on representation and diversity in literature festivals.

Clare Wigzell is a Leeds poet and feminist interested in expressing nature, place and art through physical and imaginative experiences.

Dalton Harrison found himself in prison in the words he wrote. He has never stopped writing since. He may be an ex offender but he is a poet. A trans man and a person behind it all.

Daniela Nunnari is a poet, reader, daydreamer, and telly addict, with a BA and MA in Literature, and a collection, *Red Tree* @valleypress danielanunnari.wordpress.com

Denni Turp lives in north Wales with her two rescue dogs. She likes trees, owls, books, music, art and poetry, and her poems have been published in various places.

Di Slaney runs livestock sanctuary Manor Farm Charitable Trust and publisher Candlestick Press. Second collection is *Herd Queen* (Valley Press 2020).

Doireann Ní Ghríofa is author of six critically-acclaimed books of poetry. Her awards include the Rooney Prize for Irish Literature.

Elizabeth Carola is a poet, prose-ist, science researcher. Explorer of the space between the empirical and the mysterical. Latest book *Crickets* (2020)

Emilie Lauren Jones is published with HCE Magazine, Half Moon Books and Under the Radar Magazine (Summer 2020). Commissioned by UK City of Culture. Current Dynamo mentee.

Emily Reynolds lives in Bristol with her family. She spends her days working with new mothers and writes after bedtime when everything is quiet.

Emily Rose was the first female Staffordshire Poet Laureate, is co-founder of WordCraft, and was shortlisted for Culture Recordings' New Voice in Poetry Prize 2020.

Emma Purshouse is poet laureate for the City of Wolverhampton.

Emma Storr lives in Yorkshire where the local weather dictates her mood and activities. The menopause is unpredictable and sometimes, though not always, stormy.

Federation of Writers Makar Finola Scott's poems are on posters, tapestries and postcards as well as in many magazines and anthologies. Read more at fb Finola Scott Poems

Freda Davis is inspired by nature, the seasons, mind and body, pagan and feminist themes. Her work is funny, rhythmical and musical. Good for reading aloud.

Gaia Holmes is a poet, writing tutor and pet/house sitter. She lives in Halifax in a tiny flat above the tree line on the top floor of a ramshackle Georgian mansion.

Gill Lambert co-edited this book and is a published menopausal poet. She's waiting to feel Bloody Amazing.

Gillian Mellor lives next to the West Coast Mainline and helps to run The Moffat Bookshop, an ongoing re-homing books project. She wishes everyone well through these strange times.

Hannah Hodgson, a 22 year old poet living with life limiting illness, has work published by the Poetry Society, and Teen Vogue amongst others. She received a Northern Writers Award for Poetry in 2020.

Hannah Stone is widely published in journals and anthologies and has four volumes of poetry in print. London born, lives in Leeds. Convenes poetry events, collaborates with other poets and composers.

Helen Ivory is a poet and visual artist. Her fifth Bloodaxe collection *The Anatomical Venus* examines how women have been portrayed as 'other'. She edits IS&T and teaches online for UEA/ NCW

Helen Shay writes/performs poetry from Glastonbury to golf clubs – whenever/wherever she can! She currently serves on Society of Authors Poetry & Spoken Word committee.

Hilary Robinson – wombless since 1987, writes in Saddleworth. Published in journals and anthologies, she's working towards her first pamphlet. She writes relationships.

Izzy Brittain is a Yorkshire based working class witch artist. Passionate about community, creativity & collaboration, she works with poetry & dance in diverse contexts.

J V Birch lives in Adelaide. She has three chapbooks with Ginninderra Press, one of which is about endometriosis, and a full-length collection, *More than here*.

Jacqueline Saphra's most recent collections are *Dad, Remember You Are Dead* (Nine Arches, 2019) and *Veritas: Poems after Artemisia* (Hercules Editions, 2020).

Jane Burn, a working class, ASC, bi poet & illustrator is from South Yorkshire. She now lives in the North East. Books like this are what we need more of. End the shame!

Jane Campbell is proud to be a dyke-writer living off-grid in a handmade house in rural Wales. @Maj_Ikle on twitter or https://www.facebook.com/majikle.blogspot.co.uk

Jen Hawkins is an aromatherapist, lover of words and teacher. She lives in the county of Shropshire, where the natural outstanding beauty inspires her.

Jennifer A McGowan spends more time in the 15th century than the 21st.

Jenny Robb has poems in The Morning Star; The Beach Hut, Nightingale & Sparrow, As Above so Below, *An Insubstantial Universe* anthology & forthcoming anthology *Lockdown*.

Jessica Mookherjee's second collection is called *Tigress* (Nine Arches 2019). She has been menstruating since she was 11 and has a tendency to overshare.

Jhilmil Breckenridge is a poet, writer and activist. Her poetry collection, *Reclamation Song*, was published in May 2018 by Red River Press, India and in November 2019 by Verve Poetry Press, UK.

Josie Moon is a poet, performer and community arts practitioner based in NE Lincolnshire. She loves the sea, gardens and big skies of the east coast. www.josiemoon.co.uk

Julia Webb is a poetry editor for Lighthouse & a poetry tutor. She has two collections with Nine Arches Press: *Bird Sisters* (2016) & *Threat* (2019). She lives in Norwich.

Julie Darling performs her poetry and music with the Celtic harp. She has performed in the USA and UK, eg. Arts Council England project on poetry and music for wellbeing.

Karen Hodgson Pryce lives in Aviemore. Her poetry is in Lighthouse, Northwords Now, Black Bough and Butcher's Dog. She won 3rd Prize in the Café Writers Competition 2019.

Karen Little (kazvina) is a fan of producing art and words. On occasion, she can't resist inflicting them on people outside the confines of Trailer Kaz.

Kate Noakes' most recent collection is *The Filthy Quiet*, (Parthian 2019). She lives in London and acts as a trustee for writer development organisation, Spread the Word.

Kathleen Jones lives in the Lake District, writes books, mentors students, and digs her allotment. She has 4 children and a lot of grandchildren.

Kathleen Strafford's first collection is titled *Her Own Language*. Her second collection, *Wilderness of Skin* was published by Yaffle. www.runciblespoon.co.uk

Katy Ewing is a writer and artist in South Scotland who is widely published in magazines & anthologies and was Wigtown Poetry Competition Fresh Voice Award winner 2018.

Laura Taylor has two collections published with Flapjack Press, *Kaleidoscope* and *Fault Lines*. You may find her here: https://fb.me/LauraTaylorPoet

Lesley Quayle is a poet, editor, co-founder of 4Word poetry press and a folk/blues singer.

Linda Goulden tries to summon up the energy to grow old disgracefully. Meanwhile the *Speaking Parts* come in pamphlet form, direct from herself or from Half Moon Books.

Lorna Faye Dunsire is a proud contributor to Beautiful Dragons' anthologies – a big Brontë fan – daughter of poets – politically expressive – mental health professional.

Louise Dunsire is a regular April poet and a grandmother of 1 year, watching motherhood from a safe distance and marvelling at the skill of it all!

Lucy Jeynes Writer. Poet. Supermum. Chatterbox. Asked a friend to describe her in one sentence and he said seems quite posh but always has gravy on her chips.

Lydia Unsworth has published two collections, and her latest pamphlet *Yield* is out now from KFS Press. Twitter: @lydiowanie

Lytisha Tunbridge would forget her head if it wasn't screwed on. Luckily she remembers to update her website lytishapoet.co.uk/ & hosts poetryaloudpresents.com/.

Maeve McKenna is from Ireland. Her poetry has been placed in many international poetry competitions, published widely online and in print. Writing is her route out.

Maggie Mackay's pamphlet *The Heart of the Run* is published by Picaroon Poetry with her full collection *A West Coast Psalter* due out early 2021. She loves to daydream.

Mandy Macdonald is well past the menopause (phew) and writing more than ever. Her debut pamphlet is *The Temperature of Blue* (www.bluesalt.co.uk). She does music, too.

Marg Roberts, poet & novelist loves writing and reading. Other passions: family, friends, cycling, walking & gardening. Website: http://www.margroberts.co.uk

Margaret Rowland was born in Derbyshire, matured in Sheffield, retired to Spain. I'm back reciting poetry in the North. Most days a curve ball arrives to inspire my writing.

Maria Andrews is a lost soul searching for poet colonies to call home. When not writing she makes films, art, improvises dance and is a passionate lesbian lover.

Marion Oxley was recently shortlisted for Cheltenham Festival's 'Wild' Poem Competition and the Erbacce Poetry Prize. She has worked in mental health, amongst other jobs.

Martha Flower aspires to be a fearless creative and force for good in the world. This is her first time published and she's thrilled to be part of this project.

Maya Chowdhry's work explores worldly justice. Her poetry collections are: *The Seamstress and the Global Garment*, (Crocus Press 2009) and *Fossil*, (Peepal Tree Press 2016).

Melanie Branton's collections are *Can You See Where I'm Coming From?* (Burning Eye, 2018) and *My Cloth-Eared Heart* (Oversteps, 2017). She lives in North Somerset.

Miranda Lynn Barnes is a poet, writer, and librarian from the US, now living in the UK. Her debut poetry pamphlet, *Blue Dot Aubade*, is forthcoming in 2020 from V. Press.

Moira Garland's prize-winning poetry is published in magazines and anthologies, including The North, and forthcoming in Poetry Space, and Yaffle Press. @moiragauthor

Morag Smith thought poetry would be less time consuming than novel and short story writing then discovered it wasn't. She has been widely published in magazines and anthologies.

Olivia Tuck's pamphlet *Things Only Borderlines Know* is out now with Black Rabbit Press. Find her on Twitter: @livtuckwrites

Pam Thompson is a writer and lecturer based in Leicester. Her latest publication is *Strange Fashion* (Pindrop Press, 2017). She is a 2019 Hawthornden Fellow.

Pat Edwards hosts Verbatim poetry open mic and curates Welshpool Poetry Festival. Her debut pamphlet was *Only Blood* (Yaffle 2019). *Kissing in the Dark* is due out with Indigo Dreams in 2020.

Paula Dunn is a Yorkshire based artist whose atmospheric paintings are inspired by the weather and its impact on the landscape (www.pauladunnartist.com).

Penny Blackburn lives in the North East, although she is originally from Yorkshire and it shows. She writes poetry/fiction around her full-time job as a teacher in FE.

Penny Sharman is a published poet, photographer & artist. She is inspired by wild landscapes and spirituality.web: pennysharman.co.uk

Rachael Smart writes essays, poetry and short fiction. Recent work has been published at The Letters Page, Vol 5 and Unthology 11.

Rachel Burns is widely published in journals and anthologies. Her debut poetry pamphlet, *A Girl in a Blue Dress* is published by Vane Women Press.

Rachel Davies, prize winning poet and first Spawn of the Dragon, will have her first pamphlet, *Every Day I Promise Myself*, published in Dec 2020 with 4Word Press.

Rebecca Bilkau co-edited this book, founded Beautiful Dragons Collaborative Press – her latest pamphlet is *Sunday's Child* (Wayleave Press 2020). She aspires to be blithe.

Rebecca Gethin has written 5 poetry publications. *Vanishings* has just been published by Palewell Press.

Rosemary McLeish (rosemarymcleish.co.uk), prize-winning poet, published widely in journals & anthologies has 2 collections published by Wordsmithery, working on a 3rd.

S M Jenkin, second generation Irish poet and cheese addict has published in Anti-Heroin Chic, Boyne Berries, Confluence, Dissonance & The Interpreter's House. Up Mayo!

Sandra Burnett is an Otley Poet. Her poems have been widely published. Her pamphlet *New Lease* and collection *Between Sea and Sky* are published by Half Moon Books, Otley.

Sarah L Dixon lives in a Huddersfield valley. Inspiration comes from pubs, music, being by and in water and adventures with her son, Frank. http://thequietcompere.co.uk/

Sarah Miles is a poet, editor and writer from Tunbridge Wells. She has been published in various books and websites and runs Paper Swans Press.

Sarah Wragg has been breathing Beautiful Dragon poetic fire for many years. Watch out at Halloween - if you dare - for her spooky debut collection *Ghost Walk*.

Sharon Larkin's books include *Interned at the Food Factory* (Indigo Dreams, 2019) and *Dualities* (Hedgehog Press, due 2020) http://sharonlarkinjones.com

Sheila Jacob was born and raised in Birmingham and lives in North Wales with her husband. She has three children and five grandchildren.

Shelley Tracey's poetry collection *Elements of Distance* is about finding words when it seems impossible. So is the rest of her work and her life. No silencing allowed.

Sheryl McMahon lives in West Yorkshire. A member of Otley Poets, she writes poetry to try and make sense of life's ups and downs. Occasionally, she reaches her goal.

Siobhan Mac Mahon is an award-winning Irish Poet & Word Witch whose poetry celebrates the return of the Sacred Feminine and our deep connection to the Earth.

Stella Wulf can't walk on water, but she can feed a crowd on 5 loaves & 5 fishes, turn wine into water, and wear white pants. A second coming? That would be a bloody miracle

Su Ryder has had work published in the Anthology *And The Stones Fell Open*, and Strix magazine. Su also performs her poetry at open mics, and writes short fiction.

Sue Hubbard is a poet, novelist, and art critic. She has published 3 collections of poetry and 3 novels. Her latest, *Rainsongs*, is published by Duckworth.

Sue Mackrell writes about hidden histories, witches and women's issues. Her poems have been displayed in Leicester women's toilets. See www.ekphrastic.net for more!

Susannah Violette a Pushcart Prize nominee, has had poems placed or commended in various prizes and appears in many publications worldwide.

Tina Cole is a Black Country wench, poet, gardener. Winner of the Yaffle Poetry Competition 2020. Organiser of annual Young People's Poetry Competition – youngpeoplespoetry.org

Tonnie Richmond was a social scientist. She is a keen amateur archaeologist and only took up writing poetry after she retired and moved to Leeds.

Tracey Rhys is a Welsh writer and copy editor. Her pamphlet *Teaching a Bird to Sing* was published in 2016. She has worked as a poet in theatre and publishes in journals.

Tricia Marcella Cimera is a Midwestern (USA) poet with a worldview. Her work can be found in places ranging from the Buddhist Poetry Review to The Ekphrastic Review.

Victoria Bennett is an award-winning writer, full-time carer, mother, juggler of chronic illness and founder of Wild Women Press. Published by Indigo Dreams. www.beewyld.co.uk

Victoria Riddiford is a Bristol-based counsellor and Writing for Wellbeing practitioner. She has never shared her work publicly before, so she's excited to be in print.

Wendy-Jane Walton is a running granny, dreamer, retired GP and writer. She has had essays and poems published in medical journals and *These are the Hands* anthology

Yvonne Ugarte is 61 years old. She has written poetry since age 5 and appeared in several anthologies. Children's book of poetry to be published in 2020.

D r a g o n Y a f f l e

2020
a rare coupling of

YAFFLE

and

Beautiful Dragons Press

38300 Wolfenbüttel Germany

All poems © their respective author
Design by Rebecca Bilkau

ISBN:978-1-913122-16-4.